D1479476

Gross/Lieberknecht/Dresden

Alt Dressden.

DRESDEN

Text Reiner Gross
Photographs by
Werner Lieberknecht

Edition Leipzig

Kindly sponsored by Dresdner Bank AG Dresden.

English translation by Victor Dewsbery

Die deutsche Bibliothek – CIP Einheitsaufnahme

Dresden / Text Reiner Gross. Photogr. by Werner
Lieberknecht. Engl. transl. by Victor Dewsbery –
Leipzig: Ed. Leipzig, 1997
Dt. Ausg. u.d.T.
ISBN 3-361-00478-0

© 1997 by Edition Leipzig
Duplication of the texts and illustrations in whole
or in part without the permission of the publisher
is a violation of copyright and a punishable offence.
This includes any reproduction, translation,
recording on microfilm or processing with any
electronic system.
Cover design: Morian & Bayer-Eynck, Coesfeld
Translation: Victor Dewsbery, Berlin
Layout: Dietmar Kunz
Reproduction: Satz Repro Grafik, Leipzig
Typography: XYZ-Satzstudio, Naumburg
Printed by Jütte Druck, Leipzig
Printed in Germany

Printed on non-ageing paper made with
chlorine-free bleached cellulose

Contens

Foreword

Dresden can be regarded as a young city. At present, it is preparing to celebrate the eight hundredth anniversary of its first documentary record in 2006. This is underlined by a comparison with Regensburg, which is a full one thousand years older, and with the nearby Meissen, which has existed for over one thousand years. Our Slavic settlement area of Nisani (Lowlands) only saw systematic land conquest in the course of the German eastward expansion after 1150. This led to settlements being founded with German names, but some Slavic names were also preserved. Thus, the settlement "drezdane" (marsh forest people) on the right bank of the Elbe gave the name "Dresden" to the new town which was founded on the left bank. But Slavic remnants are not only found in place names with typical endings such as "itz" and "witz", they are also preserved in surnames and in Saxon dialect phrases. For example, Saxons still say "Hitsche" for a footstool, "Mutzel" for fluff, and they express affirmation with the word "nu", which stems from the Czech word for yes, "ano".

Thus, Dresden and its populace are the product of many influences. The city and people received a wide variety of impulses because of the position at the meeting point of the warm Catholic south and the sober Protestant north, the Romantic west and the Slavic east. For centuries learned people, artists, musicians, poets and merchants were attracted to the city on the Elbe – and went from Dresden to places throughout Europe and all over the world.

Dresden also earned itself a prominent place in economic history. It was the site of the first German long distance railway, a centre of the German chocolate and tobacco industry and a production centre for fine mechanical and optical goods. Brand names and products from Dresden conquered the market: Odol, Melitta, condensed milk, the first reflex camera in the world and the world-famous Meissen Porcelain, which was invented in Dresden. A local law of 1878 created a far-sighted framework for siting industries outside the inner city and the bourgeois residential suburbs. Thus, the growing metropolis was able to preserve the flair of a well-preserved residence city with a continuing cultural tradition.

Today, Dresden is the capital of the Free State of Saxony, one of the federal states of Germany. The people of Dresden make use of the opportunities of their new freedom throughout the world – but especially in and for their city. There are many legends about the peculiarities of the people of Dresden. It is said that they prefer to remain in the background, that they always start sums by calculating the places after the decimal point, that they are gullible and can be easily tricked. But they are also reputed to be adaptable and creative, tolerant and open-minded. And their love of their home, their boundless allegiance to their city – lifelong and wherever they settle – is undisputed throughout the world. Their love of the city is so intense that they bear within themselves an image of the maltreated, ravaged and devastated city as a realistic counterpart to a transformed romantic image. Happy the city which bears such descendants, and happy the person who has such an emotional loyalty to his city.

Dresden is now in a process of rapid transformation. Desire and necessity provide a dual motivation for the people of Dresden day after day, characterising the face of its urban identity. Traditional and innovative areas of activity arise and must be mastered. The world is already visiting the city – not waiting for its anniversary. Visitors arrive here every day: business travellers, tourists, newcomers, investors. A modern infrastructure is being developed. Sometimes the development is too hectic, sometimes it is over-conservative. However, it can certainly be said that the Dresden coat of arms today should bear a building crane instead of the Meissen lion. This situation is full of potential, but it also involves great dangers. The people of Dresden do not take it lightly, because the face of their city is also part of their own identity – at home and in the far-flung corners of the world.

Matthias Griebel

Dresden
then and now

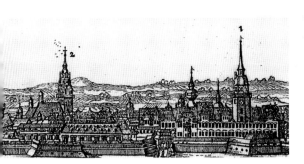

Today, visitors to Dresden – whether they are business travellers, company representatives, tourists or just passing through – arrive in the Saxon regional capital on the Elbe by plane, long-distance bus or private car, and rarely by train. Even before humanity was blessed with these modern means of transport, there were already numerous visitors to the city – merchants, crafts apprentices, emigrants from other states, art enthusiasts and people who hoped to find happiness and make a career in this major city of Saxony. The daily announcements of "Arriving and departing persons" in the Dresden Chronicle from the end of the 18th century onwards are an eloquent testimony to this flow of visitors. All of them arrived either by stagecoach, in their own carriages, by horse or on foot. But however travellers arrived in the city then or arrive there now, they are always met by the view of the gracious scenery of the river valley of the upper Elbe, with the residential area to the right and left of a great meander in the river, framed on the right bank of the river by vineyard slopes from Hoflössnitz to Pillnitz and by the parts of Dresden Heath which touch the city, and in a greater expanse on the left bank by the ridges of the eastern Erzgebirge mountains, the Plauen valley and the fertile slopes stretching downstream towards Meissen. This geographical and scenic setting produces a warm climate, especially as a result of the Elbe valley basin and the temperatures in the city, which are about two or three degrees above those in the surrounding uplands. That in turn favours the flora and fauna, which is clearly shown in the numerous parks and gardens and the tree-lined roads which are found even in the centre of the city. This natural environment enabled Dresden to develop over many centuries to become one of the most beautiful cities on earth. The Russian poet and novelist, Aleksei Konstantinovich Tolstoi (1817–1875), wrote from Nepal on 25th December 1863 to his intimate friend in Dresden, Karolina Pavlova (1807–1893): "I tell you without any flattery that I only know one city on earth where I could live, and that city is Dresden. Not that I am insensitive to the splendour of the cities of Italy, but in them I do not find that moral atmosphere of the streets and houses, if we disregard the inhabitants, which presumably contains ingredients in Dresden which are necessary for my psychological lungs."

This beautiful city, which was known in the 18th century as the "Florence of the North", has frequently suffered at the hands of Fate in the many centuries of its history. There were great fires in the Altstadt (old part of the city) in 1491 and in the Neustadt (new part of the city) in 1685. Each time, almost the entire city had to be rebuilt. Major destruction was caused by military disputes such as the Seven Years War from 1756 to 1763 and in the Napoleonic Era. During the former war, the city burned in 1758 and 1759, and canon attacks in 1760 and 1763

reduced half of Dresden to ruins. The Prussian bombardment of July 1760 was particularly destructive. The Kreuzkirche (Church of the Cross) and 416 houses were destroyed by Prussian canons which were set up around the city. At the beginning of the war, Dresden had a population of about 63,000, in 1763 there were only about 44,000 inhabitants. When Goethe visited the city in 1768 "to see a great number of major works of art at once" – which was again possible because the paintings which had been stored in Königsstein during the war had by then been returned – he also saw the ruins from the Prussian bombardment of 1760. The 29-year old writer commented: "These precious experiences which prepare the mind and soul for true art were, however, interrupted and dampened by one of the saddest moments, by the destroyed and desolate state of so many of Dresden's streets through which I passed. The ruins of Mohrenstrasse and the broken spire of the Kreuzkirche (Church of the Cross) made a deep impression on me, and they are still a dark shadow before my mind's eye. From the dome of the Frauenkirche (Church of Our Lady), I saw these pitiable ruins strewn among the beautiful urban scene." The Kreuzkirche was rebuilt in 1792, 32 years after it had been destroyed.

The battles of 1813 were so severe that a tenth of the inhabitants did not survive the year. The "Diary of a Dresden citizen" by Taggesell reports that there was a perma-nent movement of troops through the city with forced billeting for alternating armies, battles and destruction. This was particularly so because Dresden was an important strategic fortress and, at the same time, a hospital city. In 1813, the houses of Dresden's citizens had to bear the unspeakable burden of 7,376,947 billet days for soldiers from many nations. In the days of revolution in September 1830 and May 1849, many inner city buildings were also destroyed, such as the old opera house by the Zwinger rampart.

But the greatest disaster befell the city on 13th and 14th February 1945. This was the "Zero" hour in the history of a city which had an impressive past over many centuries in art, culture, architecture, and sometimes even in politics and commerce. The centre of the seventh largest city in Germany, which had a population of 630,000 in 1945 and even today has 200,000 fewer inhabitants, was reduced to rubble and ashes in just a few hours. The church clocks in the city had just struck 10 on the evening of 13th February 1945 when the first squadrons of the Royal Air Force unleashed their bombs. Within the next 20 minutes, the area from Albertplatz in the Neustadt (new part of the city) to the main station was pounded by 3000 high explosive bombs, 2500 fire bombs, 400,000 incendiary devices and 100 air mines. Hans Nadler, who is now over 90 and the longest serving specialist on the conservation of Saxon monuments, described the ensuing situation as follows: "The fire roared through the city like a storm, and it burned up all the oxygen…" Three hours later, the second attack came on 14th February from 1:23 to 1:52 in the morning, and the third attack followed at midday from 12:15 to 12:25. After that, the inner city of Dresden within the famous "26" circular route consisted only of rubble, of ruins towering into a melancholy February sky, of hidden and melted street lanterns, tram lines and steel structures.

In view of the total destruction of the city, the ageing Gerhard Hauptmann, the author of plays which were performed in the Dresden theatre by a leading German drama ensemble right up to the declaration of "total war" in 1944, wrote the following words:

"Anyone who has forgotten how to weep will learn it again at the destruction of Dresden. This bright morning star of youth was a light to the world. I know that there are enough good spirits in England and America to whom the Sixtine Madonna was not unknown and who weep with pain at the passing of this star. I personally experienced the destruction of Dresden under the Sodom and Gommorah hell of enemy planes.

When I say 'experienced', it still seems like a miracle. I do not consider myself so important to believe that fate could have expressly reserved this horror for me at this very place in the part of my world which is almost the most cherished.

I stand at the end of my life, and I envy all my dead comrades who were spared this experience. I weep.
Do not shrink from the word weep; the great heroes of antiquity, including Pericles and others, were not ashamed of tears.

From Dresden, from its constant and beautiful care of the musical and verbal arts, such splendid streams flowed out into the world, and even England and America thirsted to drink of them. Have they forgotten?

I am almost 83, and I stand before God with my heritage which, alas, is powerless and comes only from the heart; it is the plea that God should love, refine and purify people more for their salvation than he has up to now."

The Dresden photographer, Karl Peter, recorded the destruction in pictures with a Leica camera in spite of the prohibition by the police. Years later, these photographs went around the world and bore testimony to the unspeakable destruction of a first-class city of art and culture.

The Dresden of the present is no longer the Dresden of the "Zero" hour. Decisions about its new appearance were made in the period from 1946 to 1948, and they were systematically implemented up to the beginning of the 1980s. They were politically dictated by the SED, the East German Socialist Unity Party and were directed against "bourgeois ideology" and marked by the idea of a "Socialist city". Under Walter Weidauer, who was appointed as the governing mayor of Dresden on 8th May 1945 as the successor to Rudolf Friedrichs, the removal of rubble over large areas of the city began in the early summer of 1946, without any consideration being given to private initiatives to restore destroyed buildings and despising the individual house on its own plot of land, which had been one of the characteristic structural elements of every historically developed city in Europe. This earned Weidauer the popular nickname "Lawn Walter" because of the green expanses which dominated the face of the city after 1946 in place of the ruins, and some of which are still present today. The destruction of architectural monuments which began with the removal of bomb debris did not even spare the oldest church in Dresden, the Sophienkirche. It was only the protests, resistance and competent warnings of individuals such as Herbert Conert, Richard Konwiarz and Hans Nadler with his staff in the regional monument protection office which saved some highly important monuments, such as the Theaterplatz complex, the palace complex and the inner new city. After 1980 it was thought that the barbarian treatment of architectural monuments in the 1950s, 1960s and 1970s had been finally overcome – and then, in 1983, plans were made for the only remaining citizen's house built by Pöppelmann in Grosse Meissner Gasse to make way for the new Interhotel. Shortly before the explosive charges were attached, a broad citizens' protest movement, which transcended the boundaries of parties and beliefs, succeedeed in preventing the destruction of this unique architectural memorial of the 18th century. Today, Pöppelmann's work, which was competently restored by Dresden craftsmen in 1984/85, can be admired as the central element of the "Bellevue" maritime hotel between the Blockhaus and the Japanese Palace. The efforts in the GDR period to preserve buildings saved from demolition, which were always characterised by economic shortages, led to structural reinforcements, but they also led to the use of buildings without a complete and final restoration. Only the Schauspielhaus (theatre), Zwinger, Semper Gallery, Semper Opera and Blockhaus were completely restored. The peaceful social revolution in the GDR, which began in November 1989, started a process in Dresden which can be regarded as a "recovery" of the architectural character of the city. Even now, cranes and scaffolding around historic buildings are characteristic elements of the appearance of the city. In 2006, when the city on the Elbe celebrates the 800th anniversary of its first appearance in historical documents, the war damage caused in the Second World War to the remaining buildings from the 18th, 19th and 20th century will finally have been repaired. But the city will irrevocably have a different architectural appearance from that which brought it world renown before 1945.

But there is one thing that Dresden has never lost – and has preserved through all the difficulties, destruction and ideologically one-sided politics: its reputation as a city of the arts and the theatre, a place which upholds not only German culture but also European and world culture. Whether the city was ruled by a royal dynasty, an elected parliamentary minister-president, a governor of the Reich appointed by the Fuehrer or a 1st secretary of the district administration of the Socialist Union Party nominated by the Communist Central Committee in Berlin – the Dresden art galleries, the Dresden State Orchestra, the Dresden Philharmonic Orchestra, the Dresden Theatre, the Dresden State Opera the museums that arose from the Electoral Chambers of Art, the Saxon State Library and the Main Saxon State Archive – all of these institutions, in conjunction with the unique special character of the landscape, have determined the special nature and the flair of the metropolitan city on the River Elbe.

The city's role as a residence of the nobility and the capital of the federal state has particularly contributed to this identity. From the year 1135, when Margrave Konrad of Wettin inherited the house of Groitzsch and thus also acquired the Nisan territory, the area around the present day city of Dresden belonged to the margraviate of Meissen. The subsequent extension of a castle complex, which probably already existed, to become a margravian castle at this important trade route crossing point on the Elbe between Briesnitz downstream and Blasewitz/Loschwitz upstream and the construction work on a stone bridge across the Elbe, which has been archeologically shown to have commenced in the last third of the 12th century, mark the fixed points in the development of the city under margravian leadership. The first known seal of the city with the lion of the Mark of Meissen, the Landsberg stakes in the shield and the inscription "Sigilm Burgensium in Dresedene" shows clearly that the city was founded by the Margraves. There are no towers and battlements as symbols of municipal freedom. This geometrically planned city, which excluded the existing Slavic settlements, first acquired a wider importance beyond the local region under the rule of Margrave Heinrich the Noble (1218 – 1288). After 1274 it became the permanent residence of the Margrave, and thus for the first time the centre of government and administration in the Wettin state in the margraviate of Meissen and the landgraviate of Thuringia. This role was lost again after Heinrich died. Other cities in the margraviate of Meissen such as the free hill city of Freiberg, Leipzig or the town of Pirna with its Elbe trading rights and its Elbe trading justice exceeded Dresden in their economic importance and their population figures.

It was only the last third of the 15th century that brought the decisive change. In this period, the town acquired a new dimension in that it became the permanent residence of the Wettin Elector Ernst and his brother, Duke Albrecht, who was two years younger. After the Leipzig Partition of 1485, the city advanced to become the residence of the Albertine Duchy of Saxony, and from 1547 the residence of the Albertine Electorate of Saxony, which was founded by Moritz. From this time onwards, the development of Dresden was more closely linked with the development of the state, the ups and downs of Saxon history – and even German and European history – than other towns. This also had a decisive influence on the special character of the city. Two hundred years after the Leipzig Partition, the Privy Secretary and Archivist of the Privy Council, Anton Weck, praised the city in the first city history, printed in 1680 by Forberger in Nürnberg and published under the title "Description and Presentation of the Widely Renowned Electoral Saxon Residence and Main Fortress of Dresden." He wrote: "This place now consists of two cities under the name of Dresden, Neu-Dresden (New Dresden) and Alt-Dresden (Old Dresden). Of the two, New Dresden is preferable to the old in that it is not only realiter fortificret with high and strong ramparts, stately fortifications, casemates…, but that the fortifications are also and mainly … equipped with roomy piece stands, extremely thick double vaults and counter-mines below the earth…, so that perhaps few fortresses or none at all can be found far and wide which could exceed it in splendour and art. … This residence city is also famous because, more than all other towns in the Electorate of Saxony and the associated lands, it has a great number of splendid Electoral and princely, yea royal and other majrestic buildings, and within the city wall the town is made up of 36 alleys, large and small, and in two marketplaces it has well built private and communal houses, some of which are beautifuly designed and most with vaults below, and which are safeguarded throughout against all risk of fire with solid fire walls and are three and four storeys high and completely built of stone."

In volume 31 of Zedler's Universal Lexicon, published in 1742 in Halle and Leipzig, Dresden is described as "the Electoral Saxon residence, main fortress and main city in the entire Electorate" and as "one of the most famous cities in the whole of Germany. It lies in Meissen on the Elbe .. in a pleasant and fertile region richly blessed with grain, fruit, wine and others". The Renaissance residence which arose in the 16th century was converted to a Baroque residence after 1680, especially under August the Strong and his son, Friedrich August II. The 19th century saw Dresden develop to become the state capital which it is today, with a constant expansion, with an almost explosive growth of the population after 1830, with an unparalleled industrialisation which, after 1850, made Dresden into the centre of

important new branches of industry and an important German industrial city. The city was an administrative centre, a major junction in the German railway network, an important port for shipping on the Elbe and a centre of science and technology. All these elements continue to characterise the city even today in its buildings and its people.

If a Dresden citizen, whether he be such by birth or by choice, should lead a good friend or acquaintance through the city, it would usually be the first time for a long time that he himself is an observer and idler in the city centre. He is then always faced with the difficult choice of where to start and where to end the tour of the city, which route to take to show as much as possible while keeping more or less to the historical sequence. For a short tour, it is probably best to follow the "26" circular route. Starting at the entrance of the Hauptbahnhof (main station) looking towards Prager Strasse and the old city, the tour proceeds clockwise around the historic centre of the city: Hauptbahnhof – Freiberger Strasse – Schweriner Strasse – Marienbrücke – Neustädter Bahnhof – Albertplatz – Bautzner Strasse – Hoyerswerdaer Strasse – Albertbrücke – Sachsenplatz – Güntzstrasse – Strassburger Platz – Lennéstrasse – Hauptbahnhof. The centre of this inner city area is Schlossplatz. In one of its bumpy cobblestones, the letter "N" is engraved – N for Napoleon Bonaparte. On this Square, where the rider's

statue of King Albert is still missing, the French Emperor inspected the parade of the Grande Armée in 1812 in the presence of Emperor Franz I of Austria and King Friedrich Wilhelm II of Prussia before setting out from Dresden on 29th May to his great Russian campaign. Wilhelm von Kügelgen gave an eye witness report of those historic days: "They passed through Dresden in densely crowded masses. I still see the long, dark processions of the old guard with their proud eagles, their tall bearskin hats and the martial faces like a sombre dream. … At the beginning of May, Napoleon himself appeared and, surrounded by numerous other vassal dukes, received visits from his high allies, Emperor Franz and King Friedrich Wilhelm. … There was, in fact, a lot to be seen in Dresden in those days. The presence of so many armies filled the city with military pomp; bells and canons sounded out to greet the dukes, splendid parades and manoeuvres entertained them, and by night the city glowed in the enchanted glare of a thousand lanterns. … And all the houses were full of billeted soldiers who laughed, spoke and cursed in almost all the tongues of Europe."

At this point, which documents European history in an almost unassuming manner, we begin our tour of the old and new city of modern Dresden, a tour which will also take us to some highlights of the surrounding area. Jean Paul wrote in a letter from Bayreuth to Heinrich Voss on 25th

June 1822: "Of Dresden I will say but little
because your answer must first give me the
fire to do so. Just one thing! Everything went
and flew beautifully. Just as everything went
wrong for me in Munich down to the smal-
lest detail, so everything went well in Dresden, starting with the splendid apartment in
the freedom of all natural beauties. The
summer residence palaces have a superior
prospect to all others in Germany. The
Brühl Terrace in the evening with its lights
and hills and the bridge and the Elbe
gave me an hour of inner enchantment
which I had sought in vain – and not in
Heidelberg."

The origins
of the city

**The Residenzschloss (Residence Palace)
in Dresden**

On 31st March 1206, Dietrich the Oppressed, who was the Margrave of Meissen from 1197 until his death in 1221, issued a deed which contained in its last line but one the remark: "Acten sunt haec Dresdene." This was the first time that Dresden was mentioned in written history. A good sixty years before, when the Wettin Margrave Konrad took possession of the Nisan area as part of the inheritance of the House of Groitzsch, he had fortifications built or existing castles extended at the points which were strategically important for his rule. At the point where the structure of the terrain caused the trade route to cross from the right bank to the left bank of the Elbe, there was a margravian castle. In this castle in 1206, Dietrich the Oppressed settled a boundary argument between the Bishop of Meissen and the Burgrave Heinrich von Dohna concerning a "castellum Thorun" built by the latter on the territory of the Meissen diocese. At the invitation of the margrave, the following persons appeared in the Dresden castle complex: 17 clerical and 34 secular dignitaries as witnesses, 21 ministerial dignitaries as arbitrators and two margravian delegates and the disputing parties with their entourages. To accommodate and feed all these guests, the castle must have been a considerable size.

The Elbe crossing and castle also became the starting point for a settlement of both long-distance merchants and craftsmen. If we give credence to recent archaeological findings and older written traditions, this was also the site of a stone bridge; the start of building work on this bridge can be dated to the 12th century. The settlement by the castle, which is regarded as a margravian project, must have developed relatively quickly and become important for the margraviate. As early as 1216, a further document issued by the margrave speaks of "our city of Dresden" (Acta sunt bec … in civitas nostra Dreseden). Finally, the oldest surviving seal of the city also refers to the margravian city. The seal does not portray battlements, the city wall and city towers as the symbol of municipal freedom, instead it portrays the lion of the Mark of Meissen and the Landsberg stakes as symbols of the ducal dominion over the city, combined with the inscription "sigillum Burgensium in Dresedene". Apart from the Slavic villages on both sides of the Elbe which arose after 600, the margravian castle and the margravian city which developed next to it were the origin of the development of Dresden up to the present day. Schlossplatz and the area immediately around the palace thus form the original area of the city.

**View to the Hausmannsturm
(caretaker's tower)**

The Dresden residence palace, as a crystalisation point of the state and municipal development, has seen a turbulent history. At the

View of Dresden from the
Waldschlösschen (Forest Palace)

17

time of its origins, it was a margravian castle to safeguard German dominion at the most important Elbe crossing point in the Slavic district of Nisani. When the Wettins succeeded in 1195 in extending their dominion upstream on the Elbe from Meissen to beyond Dresden, bordering on the burgravian state of Dohna, which was a fiefdom of the state of Bohemia, the castle complex acquired an even greater strategic importance. The castle was therefore structurally extended and fortified. In 1289, the castle complex was first mentioned in a document as a "castrum", but it is certainly at least 100 years older. At the north-western corner of the castle was the Hausmannsturm (caretaker's tower), the castle keep, which was used as a residence and a place of refuge. Probably the oldest stone monument in the city today, in its form and design it goes back to the extensive construction measures under Margrave Wilhelm, to whom the margraviate of Meissen was assigned in the Chemnitz Partition. Square in shaped in the lower floors, the tower above these floors was octagonal and had a flat dome. This building, known as the "Hausmannsturm", was then a hallmark of the castle and the city from 1454 to 1461, and even in a subsequent construction phase when the castle was converted into a residence palace, initially under Elector Friedrich II and then under Elector Ernst and his younger brother Albrecht from 1468 to 1480. It was probably the ingenious architect of these Wettin rulers,

Arnold von Westfalen, who added the west wing and connected it with the Hausmannsturm by building the palace chapel. Thus, in the last third of the 15th century the palace complex developed, characterised by the four heterogeneous wings and dominated by the commanding tower in the centre of the north wing facing the Elbe. The palace tower, which regained its towering position above the roofs of Dresden in 1991, acquired its present form in the last third of the 17th century. Wolf Caspar von Klengel was appointed as the Electorate chief master builder by the Elector Johann Georg II in 1656 at the age of 26 as the successor to Wilhelm Dilich and led the structural modernisation of the residence palace after 1674. In the course of this work, the palace tower was raised to 97 metres. To this purpose, it was given a Swiss dome, a multiple curved tower dome with a lantern-like intermediate section and an open skylight. Klengel was a grandson of the Electorate's senior armourer and fortress builder, Paul Buchner, who was active in Dresden under Elector August from 1558 onwards. In Dresden's architectural history, Klengel was at the transition from Mannerism to the high Baroque. Educated in Italy, personally acquainted with the great masters Francesco Borromini and Lorenzo Bernini in Rome, Klengel himself became a teacher of renowned architects of the Augustine age in Saxony such as Johann Georg Starcke and Johan Friedrich Karcher. He also initiated

the young Prince Friedrich August into the secrets of great architecture and stimulated in him an interest in and love of architecture. Numerous sketches and designs by the later Elector of Saxony and King of Poland are still preserved, and they show that he had considerable knowledge of building. Cornelius Gurlitt, an excellent connoisseur of written documents from the days of August the Strong, wrote in 1907: "The drawings which were completed for the King were vast in number; when the Swedes were in the land and the Poles tormented him, he withdrew to the portfolios in which his architectural dreams were brought into form, in which Dresden and Warsaw were transformed into cities of splendour with no care for the cost and the available resources. For August the Strong, building was a form of expression of his royal senses, the quintessence of his rule."

The Fürstenzug (Procession of the Dukes)
If we then proceed from Schlossplatz into Auguststrasse we see before us a unique tableau of glazed tiles, 101.9 metres long and 10.51 metres high. This work of art is without equal the whole world. In a unique artistic composition, a tour is given through Saxon history in portrait-like depictions of the dukes of the Wettin dynasty who ruled Saxony from the end of the 11th century onwards, their entourage and a powerful symbolism of heraldry and plants. For example, the Emperor's crown at two points

The Hausmannsturm
(Caretaker's Tower)

refers to the times when there was a possibility that the Wettin dynasty could rise to the status of the German king or Emperor – Margrave Friedrich the Serious, the son in law of King Ludwig of Bavaria who renounced the throne in favour of Charles IV of Luxembourg, and Elector Friedrich the Wise who in 1915 refused an offer to be elected as the German king. The historical accuracy of the clothing, the armour and weapons increases the beholder's feeling that he is presented with living history. This work of art in the historical city centre, well known as the "Fürstenzug" (procession of the dukes), not only presents state history. It also symbolically expresses the close links between the development of the city and the development of the state. The two are closely connected, especially since the ruling Wettin family made Dresden their residence in the second half of the 15th century. This special status of the city is shown in the fact that the city coat of arms of Dresden is shown in the "Fürstenzug" as the thirty-fifth and last one.

A small inscription in the lower right corner at the end of the "Fürstenzug" names the creator of the work of art: Wilhelm Walther. Wilhelm Adolf Walther was born on 18th October 1826 in Cämmerwalde in the eastern Erzgebirge hills as the fourth son of a farming family. He grew up in great poverty and developed his artistic talent from an early age. At the age of 16 he left home and took up work in Zöblitz, painting landscapes on wooden boxes. With great energy he then devoted himself to studying at the Dresden Academy of the Arts. He moved to the academy in October 1843 at the age of 17 and left it twelve years later in the summer of 1855 to work independently as a historical painter, one of 22 in Dresden. His academic teachers included Ernst Rietschel, Ferdinand Anton Krüger, Johann Karl Bähr, Carl Gottlieb Peschel and Julius Hübner. Early in 1963, Gottfried Semper called him to Zurich to create a sgraffito painting on an area of 700 square metres with 45 riders and 48 persons on foot to a design by Semper. This work appears to have inspired him to embark on the design of the "long wall" of the Stallhof with its area of over 1000 square metres, because from 1861 onwards there were discussions on possible designs for the rear wall of the stable building after the sgraffito from the end of the 16th century had faded and disappeared due to weathering. At the end of 1864, Walther then submitted his designs to the academic council of the Academy of the Arts, which in turn informed the Saxon Ministry of the Interior. In April 1865, a decision was made for Walther's suggestion of a procession of dukes and the people, which was then changed by a decision of King Johann to the effect that only the procession of dukes was feasible. After further long preparations, Walter finally started to create the sgraffito painting in 1872. Day after day in wind and storm Walther, his wife, the carpenter Kern and the mason Pietsch stood on the scaffolding before the work was finally completed in the summer of 1876. It was on 21st July 1876 that the work was formally handed over to its owners. On that day, Prince Georg awarded Walther the Order of the Cross First Class of the Order of Albrecht. 62,288 marks had been paid out from the state art fund, 15,000 talers to the artist himself.

From the summer of 1876, Dresden therefore had a new work of art which was "a special adornment for the residence", as Prinz Georg, the son of King Albert and himself a later king of Saxony, expressed it. The special element was the fact that this giant painting was now freely accessible for all. But hardly a quarter of a century after the completion of the work, distinct damage to the sgraffiti was observed, caused by the climate in the Elbe valley and the increasing air pollution from combustion gases. It was soon found that the suggestions for restoration work would not be helpful. Walther's work only escaped certain destruction because of the suggestion by the Meissen porcelain manufacturing company that the painting as a whole could be tranferred to wall tiles and that these tiles could then be attached to the "long wall". After several tests in the porcelain manufacturing company, and especially after tests and discussions in the Ministry of Finance, it was decided in 1903 to transfer the wall painting to ceramic tiles. When, in March 1904, the

The Fürstenzug
(Procession of the Dukes)

Saxon parliament approved funds of 67,000 marks for 1904 and 1905, work began immediately to implement the plan. The necessary 24,000 tiles were made in 1905 and 1906, and they were fixed to the "long wall" from April to July 1907. Ten porcelain painters and other workers made the tiles, which were then fired three times in 50 large porcelain kilns.

The tile painting in gold, white and black in its glory on the wall, with the coloured coats of arms of the dominions, duchies and counties united under the Wettin dynasty, faced a literal test by fire in the night from 13th to 14th February 1945. In spite of the glowing heat in the relatively narrow Augustusstrasse and the serious structural damage to the Langer Gang, not a single tile was separated from the underlying wall. There was slight damage from bomb shrapnel which caused minor chipping and cracks. Soot-covered and blackened by smoke, in the following three decades the procession of the dukes remained in its known position because it was not possible to confiscate it and transport it away as a spoil of battle, like the works of art in the painting gallery and the Grünes Gewölbe (Green Vault). But initially it was not taken notice of in the restoration concept of the city and the state. It was only in the middle of the 1970s when the monument conservation specialists restored and reconstructed the Stallhof area and made it generally accessible to the public as a Renaissance memorial area that the procession of the dukes came more to the public attention. Thus, the work was first washed thoroughly in 1978 – not having been washed since 1939. Then, 223 tiles were replaced and 442 tiles were repaired with a special cement. On 4th October 1979, the procession of the dukes was handed over to the citizens of Dresden and their visitors in its new splendour.

On closer inspection, the beholder can recognise the margraves, dukes, Electors and kings from the House of Wettin, gathered in groups, with the rulers who dominated the historical development placed in the foreground. When the Wettin dynasty celebrated its 800th anniversary as rulers in 1889, they could justifiably point out this work with pride even though it was not created for the occasion. This is also shown by the fact that the series of rulers begins with Margrave Konrad who was made margrave of the margraviate of Meissen in 1123. It leaves out the Wettin margrave Heinrich I of Eilenburg, who became margrave of Regensburg with Meissen in 1089 and his son, Heinrich II. This was only discovered by Saxon state history research, particularly by Dr. Otto Posse, the archivist at the Saxon capital archive in Dresden in 1882. Out of respect for the work of art, it was not supplemented in 1905/1906, and there was no addition in an altered presentation to show Albert and Georg who came after King Johann.

Special mention must be made of two groups. One was centred around Margrave Heinrich the Noble, who ruled from 1221 to 1288. This was a period of great expansion of the power of the new Wettin ducal dynasty. Heinrich obtained the langraviate of Thuringia and the palatinate lands of Saxon. Under his rule, courtly and municipal life flourished. The stone bridge of the Elbe was completed in Dresden. In the last years of his rule, Heinrich selected the city on the Elbe as his permanent abode, Dresden became a residence of the ruling nobility for the first time in Saxon history. But after his death, a further 200 years passed before the city could claim to be the residence of the Wettin Electorate of Saxony.

Martin Luther in front of the Frauenkirche (Church of Our Lady)
On 31st October 1885, Dresden finally acquired a monument to the reformer and the founder of the Protestant faith, Martin Luther. The sculptor Ernst Rietschel, who was born in Pulsnitz in 1804 and advanced to great craftsmanship in Dresden, had designed a reformation memorial monument for the 350th anniversary of the Diet of Worms, which was formally dedicated in Worms in 1861. It shows the unyielding, resolute, steadfast Luther who, even in the presence of the Emperor Charles V, the German Electors and other German dignatories and the papal legates, did not re-

nounce his teachings, and on the evening of 18th April 1521 spoke the historical words: "Therefore I can and will renounce nothing because it is troublesome, unwholesome and dangerous to act against conscience. God help me. Amen."

Both during Luther's life and thereafter, the relationship between the Albertine rulers, the city and the citizens of Dresden on the one hand and Martin Luther on the other hand was not always free from problems. It is known that Luther visited Dresden twice – in the spring of 1516 and the summer of 1518 – both times at the behest of the Augustine Order, to which he belonged from 1505 onwards and for which he was the district curate. On 25th July 1518, he preached in the chapel of Dresden Palace at the invitation of Hieronymus Emser, the court chaplain of Duke Georg the Bearded. During the subsequent evening meal in Emser's house, there was a violent dispute between Emser and Luther about justification by faith, the doctrines of Thomas Aquinas and Aristotle and Luther's sermon on excommunication. That was the beginning of the animosity of Emser and other Dresden theologians towards Luther. The reformer never again set foot in Dresden.

There is a special feature of the Luther monument in Dresden. Whereas the figure of Luther is a copy of the monument in Worms, it still bears the head of the reformer as it was designed by Rietschel himself

and which the sculptor had designed for the monument in Worms. Rietschel's pupil and friend Gustav Kietz had saved the head of Luther from demolition and made it available 25 years later for the Dresden monument, which was the work of Adolf Donndorf. This statue should really have been placed in front of the Kreuzkirche (Church of the Cross) because it was there, in a celebration service on 6th July 1539 attended by the Saxon-Albertine Duke Heirich and the Saxon-Ernestine Elector Johann Friedrich the Generous, that the reformation was officially espoused in the Albertine duchy of Saxony and in its residence city. However, because the city church was at the south-eastern corner of the old market, and thus outside the market, and no architecturally suitable, beautiful site could be found for the monument to the reformer from Wittenberg, it was finally decided to place it in the new market in a location in front of the Frauenkirche (Church of Our Lady). Luther still stands there today in his courageous, defiant pose with his head held high, his right hand on the foundation of his faith and that of his followers, the Bible newly translated by him, his right foot firmly set forward to show that he has no intention of retreat. The fire bomb attack of 13th February 1945 knocked him from his pedestal, but he was not broken. He was erected again on 13th February 1955.

Behind him, the reconstruction of the Frauenkirche is now taking place, the gran-

diose task of the reconstruction in Dresden of a Baroque architectural masterpiece in faithful adherence to the details of the original. Without its unique dome, the silhouette of Dresden would not be the same as it was from the middle of the 18th century to February 1945. Apart from the Kreuzkirche (Church of the Cross), which was first named the Nikolaikirch in 1118, the Frauenkirche is the oldest church in Dresden. In the Middle Ages it was outside the city walls. Elector Moritz, who carried out the fortification of his residence, had the fortifications extended after 1546 by his fortification builder, Caspar Voigt von Wierandt, and included the Frauenkirche in the fortified city of Dresden. When the church was derelict and could no longer be saved, the city decided to demolish it and rebuild it on the same site. This was in 1722. The commission for the reconstruction was awarded to the council carpenter George Böhr, a farmer's son born in Fürstenau in the eastern Ergebirge. Again and again, Bähr rejected his own building plans until he finally found the brilliant solution in his third draft. On 26th August 1726, the foundation stone was laid for this Protestant church building which would surpass all that existed up to then. The domed central structure with seven galleries and seating for 3500, probably the most important Protestant church building in Germany, conformed particularly to the requirements of the Protestant form of service. On 27th May 1743, five years after Bähr's death, the

Memorial statue of Martin Luther in front of the ruins
of the Frauenkirche (Church of Our Lady)

spindle, knob and cross were mounted on the stone dome, thus completing the reconstruction of the church. The bombs from Prussian canons on 19th July 1760 did not harm the dome. But it did not withstand the ruinous fire on 13th/14th February 1945 after the films from the Reich Air Ministry, which were in storage in the church, had helped to multiply the heat of the fire inside the church. For over four decades, the rubble heap at the centre of Dresden was a memorial warning against war, destruction and human suffering, and in the 1980s it also became a symbol of the wish for democracy and personal freedom. Now, the Frauenkirche is being reconstructed in accordance with the will of the people of Dresden and the friends of Dresden throughout the world, financed especially by large-scale donation campaigns, commendably organised by the Dresdner Bank. In February 2006, when the dome of the Frauenkirche is completed and again marks the silhouette of the city, the use of old and new sandstone blocks will be an external and visible sign of the organic combination of the old and the new.

In search of the history of the House of Wettin

Stallhof (Stable Court)

It does not matter in which direction the beholder walks along the Fürstenzug (procession of the dukes) – at either end of this imposing work of art the visitor can pass through to the other side of this 100 metre long wall, either through Georgentor gate or through the gate between the Johanneum and the Fürstenzug. The visitor then enters the structure which even today is called the Stallhof (stable court), even though the original complex of buildings no longer exists.

At the end of the Schmalkaldic War, the young Albertine duke Moritz, a political adherent of Emperor Charles V from about 1545 onwards, was awarded the title of Elector of Saxony from the hand of the Emperor. In anticipation of the impending military confrontation with the Schmalkaldic League, the defence organisation of the Protestant estates of the Empire, Moritz, who had been allied under the protection of the Schmalkaldic League since 1537, had his most important cities refortified, especially Dresden and Leipzig. Well-fortified castle buildings, disguised as hunting palaces, arose around Dresden. After he became the Elector, this building programme was vigorously continued. Even in 1547, fundamental conversion and extension work began on Dresden Palace. Famous builders were fetched to Dresden such as Hans von Dehn-Rothfelser and Caspar Voigt von Wierandt, and also the Italians Benedikt and Gabriel

Tola from Brescia for the sgraffiti and the wall paintings. When Moritz died of the effects of a wound in July 1553 at a military encampment outside Peine, his younger brother August continued the work. In his thirty-three year rule, the Albertine Electorate became an economically flourishing, well administered and examplary German territorial state. That was shown in the fact that Elector August had a separate building constructed next to the palace for his central administrative authorities by the master builder Hans Irmisch in the years 1565 and 1566, the Kanzleihaus (chamber house). There, the Privy Council, which was created in 1574 as a completely new and innovative central administrative body of equal partners, found its home. Nevertheless, the space between the palace and the new city fortifications was architecturally rather unattractive. In a cultural history of Dresden dating from 1909, this is described in the following words: "For to the east of the palace, which then only reached to the Georgentor Gate, it was nothing less than beautiful in appearance. There still stood a section of the mediaeval city wall; in the Zwinger, i.e. in the land between the old and new city wall, piteous residences and workshops of craftsmen were found; the new market and the adjacent Moritzstrasse were not yet completely built, and the outer fortifications also still had a gap to the east facing the Elbe."

In February 1586, after the death of Elector August, his oldest surviving son became

The Stallhof (Stable Court)

the successor to his father. With him and his influential Privy Counsellor Nikolas Krell, who soon rose to be the sole ruling Chancellor, a phase of early absolutist development began in Electoral Saxony. This was also shown in the representational requirements of the Elector. On 6th June 1586, the foundation stone was laid for the stable building, the "Electoral military stable" which accommodated 128 horses and the Stallhof (stable court), which was completed along the wall section of the old city wall with the Langer Gang (long corridor). In this way, the gap between the Georgentor Gate and the Jüdenhof (Jewish court) was closed. For this purpose, the Elector purchased 24 citizens' houses, and over 2000 workers were involved in the building work which costed a total of over 200,000 Talers. This enormous building project was completed after five years. The space created between the Langer Gang, the stable building, the watering place and the chamber house was converted into a site for tournaments and other entertainments. On the narrow strip of over 100 metres in length, equestrian ring spearing, jousting, animal contests and chivalrous games were held. Two bronze columns which were erected in 1588 for ring spearing are still preserved.

The court side of the Langer Gang, which the visitor can again admire in all its splendour, is particularly attractive and architecturally successful. Twenty-two open round-arched arcades in Tuscan style can be

seen. It was Giovanni Maria Nosseni from Lugano who designed the arcade gallery on the model of Italian palaces. Above the arcade arches, similar to the Fürstenzug (procession of the dukes), are the coats of arms of the dominions, counties and territories which were acquired after 1089 by the Wettin dynasty and after 1485 by the Albertine Wettin dynasty.

These wall paintings by Heinrich Göding were added again between 1976 and 1979 after the Langer Gang had been rebuilt and restored. The long room over the arcades served as an ancestral gallery up to the 18th century, and from 1731 to 1945 as an armoury gallery for the Wettin dynasty.

The entire building complex will soon be complete, and the Saxon Renaissance architecture from the second half of the 16th century will be shown in its unique beauty. The Kanzleihaus (chamber house) will be rebuilt within the next two years and will then serve as an administrative building for the Catholic diocese of Dresden-Meissen. The city will then have a new experience in the reconstruction of important historical buildings – the reconstruction true to historical detail of a building which no longer existed.

Stable building

The stable building facing the Jüdenhof (Jewish court) had a changeable history after its construction – this applied both to its use and to later structural alterations.

It was used as a stable in the 17th century, then August the Strong had the building converted by the architect Johann Georg Maximilian von Fürstenhof between 1722 and 1725. The Elector wished to combine in this building the growing collection of paintings which were housed in the Dresden Palace and other palaces. That was the birth of the painting gallery, which was accommodated here until the Semper Museum building was opened in 1855. The same architect created a prestigious entrance by placing the beautiful double-flight English stairs in front of the building. Only a few years later, Knöffel again altered the building between 1744 and 1746, adapting it better to the requirements of a gallery. Winckelmann and Goethe, diplomats, royal visitors and the common citizens were then able to view the masterpieces of European painting of the 15th to 17th century. August the Strong purchased pictures by Wouwermann, Rubens, Jordaens, van Dyck, Rembrandt and Italian masters. In 1723, 21 pictures came to Dresden from Prague, and in 1725 and 1731, 62 and 52 pictures respectively came mainly from Italy. August's son and successor Friedrich August II, who had a great understanding for art, dramatically increased this purchasing policy, and in 1742 he purchased no less than 715 pictures. Whole collections were acquired in Italy and brought to Dresden, including the world-famous collection of Duke Francesco III of Modena. Three years previously, the

The Johanneum at Jüdenhof
(now the Museum of Transport)

Wallenstein painting collection had also come to Dresden in the same way. In 1742, the painting collection comprised 4708 pictures.

After the paintings were moved to the Semper gallery, the stable building was rebuilt towards the end of the life of King Johann to become the Museum Johanneum, which was completed in 1876. The head state master builder who carried out this work, Karl Moritz Haenel, was a contemporary of Gottfried Semper, and like Semper he remained faithful to the Renaissance concept in his design of the facade.

Shortly after the construction of the stable building, the Jüdenhof (Jewish court), the area in front of the Johanneum in which the History Museum and part of the porcelain collection was housed and which has been used as a transport museum since its reconstruction in 1957, witnessed an execution which shocked half of Europe. Under Elector Christian I, Electoral Saxon politics under the most influential Chancellor, Nikolaus Krell, were inclined towards the Calvinist parts of the Empire. This political approach, which was also called the Second Reformation, ended abruptly with the early death of Christian I on 25th September 1591. Four weeks later, Krell was arrested, interrogated, tortured and taken to the Königstein. Elisabeth of England, Henri IV of France and Wilhelm of Hessia pleaded for Krell and requested his release. The release order obtained from the Imperial Court by

Krell's wife was ignored in Saxony. On 29th September, Krell was publicly executed with a sword on the open space in front of the stable building. Even today, the place where the scaffold stood is marked with a large stone framed with smaller cobblestones and bearing the letters Kr.

The gate of the former Schlosskapelle (Palace Chapel)

Directly next to the Johanneum, to the left of it when seen from the front, is a gate in a beautiful Renaissance style. North of the Alps, and particularly in Dresden, there are not many such testimonies to the architectural achievements of this era in art which are preserved in their original condition. Even though this splendid portal has lost the brilliant colours which made it known, in the 16th century, as the Golden Gate, it still witnesses to high art and culture. This unique building is the former entrance portal of the Schlosskapelle (palace chapel) which was built in 1555 by Júan Maria from Padua, who had been called to Dresden by Elector Moritz of Saxony for his major alteration work on the palace. Two pairs of Corinthian columns on high pedestals bear a richly structured entabulature with a beautifully decorated frieze. Above it is an attica which portrays the resurrection of Christ. Next to that, in the recesses, are Isaiah on the left and Paul on the right, and above them the resurrected Christ with a flag, flanked by two statues, on the left faith with

a chalice, on the right strength with a pillar. In the recesses between the pillars are Johzn the Baptist on the left and, below him, John the Evangelist, and to the right Moses with Peter below him. The wooden door is also preserved, but at present it has been removed by the state conservation agency. Made in 1556, above the door it bears the inscription of the Protestant parts of the Empire, which was first borne on armbands at the Diet of Speyer in 1527: VDMIE = Verbum Domini Manet In Aeternum: The Word of God Remains for ever. Art history research once characterised this portal as by far "the most noble portal composition of the entire German Renaissance which, in the beauty of its proportions, the clarity of its composition, the grace of its ornaments and the agility of the divisions proclaims the spirit of the fully formed High Renaissance." This portal was a symbol of the Lutheran Reformation which entered Dresden in 1539 and for which, in the last resort, Elector Moritz stood after 1548. For that reason, he had a new chapel built in the palace in 1549 to conform to the Protestant faith, modelled on the first Protestant church building in Hartenfels Palace in Torgau, which Luther himself had consecrated in 1544.

After the Saxon Elector Friedrich August I and his son Friedrich August II converted to Catholicism, Friedrich August II had Protestant services moved from the palace chapel to the neighbouring Sophienkirche (St. Sophie's Church). That was in 1737.

After that, the palace chapel was completely rebuilt, thus extinguishing a centre of the Lutheran faith. The portal was moved to the Sophienkirche and stood there until 1864. After the neo-Gothic alteration of the Sophienkirche, the palace chapel portal was moved to the Jüdenhof (Jewish court), which is where it still stands today. It is possible that it may be returned to its original site after the reconstruction of the Dresden Palace.

The Catholic Hofkirche (court church)

In an excellent architectural position in the middle of Dresden is a building of a special type with a special history: the Catholic Hofkirche, today the cathedral of the Catholic diocese of Dresden-Meissen. Alongside the Zwinger it is the most striking Baroque monumental building that is still preserved. It is an unusual fact that in the residence city of the mother country of the Reformation and the leading Protestant part of the Empire, a Catholic church of this size could be built, with the clerical importance which is expressed in the building. Its construction is closely linked with a phase in Saxon history in which the Electorate of Saxony strove to achieve a position of power in Europe. Within the region, this period is known as the "Augustine age" in Electoral Saxony. In this period from 1694 to 1763, Dresden flourished to an outstanding degree in architecture, population development, economy, art and science, and it still has this reputation today. The two Elector-kings Friedrich August I, known as August the Strong, and his son Friedrich August II had a decisive influence on this development.

After the sudden and unexpected death of his older brother, Elector Johann Georg IV on 27th April 1694, Friedrich August took over the position of ruling Elector. When the Polish king Johann Sobieski died on 17th June 1696 and a successor had to be elected during the following year, the twenty-six year old member of the Wettin dynasty saw a chance which would not come again soon – the chance to become a king. In order to be a serious candidate for the election, he had to assume the Catholic faith. This was demanded by Poland itself, by Emperor Leopold who supported the election and by the Roman Curia. Friedrich August's cousin, Duke Christian of Saxony-Zeitz, had converted to Catholicism and held the office of Bishop of Raab in Hungary. On 2nd June 1697 in Christian's apartment in Baden near Vienna, Friedrich August received absolution from his relative and received Mass under the Roman Catholic liturgy. For the first time for 158 years, a ruling member of the Wettin dynasty thus belonged to the Catholic faith. After the election of Friedrich August as the king of Poland on 26th June 1697 on the election field outside Warsaw, the change of religion was announced and was received with great consternation in Electoral Saxony. And when his legitimate son of the same name also converted to the Catholic faith on 17th October 1717, a few days after the 200th anniversary of the beginning of the Reformation, there was uproar in Dresden, which was repeated in 1726. The Dresden superintendent, Valentin Ernst Löscher, was the leading exponent of the opposition, but as a result of the assurance of continued practice of the Protestant faith, this opposition did not develop further. Later on, the relationship between the Catholic ruling family and the Protestant Lutheran populace was marked by tolerance.

However, this conversion to the Catholic faith meant that Catholic services had to be held for the members of the Catholic faith at the Electoral court – in 1724, for example, there were over 400, and the number of Catholics living in Dresden was already about 5000. First of all, a room in the palace was equipped as a chapel. In 1707, August the Strong had the empty opera house behind the palace equipped as a larger chapel. It remained for his son, Elector Friedrich August II, to have a separate church built for the constantly growing Catholic community. It was to be the only monumental building constructed in Dresden during his rule. After lengthy preparations, construction began in 1739 under the leadership of the Italian architect, Gaetano Chiaveri. August III had personally got to know this architect, who had previously been in service in Russia under Peter the Great, in Warsaw. It was a

The Catholic Hofkirche (Court Church)

conscious decision not to commission the state master builders of the Saxon building authority with the task. With Chiaveri, Italian construction engineers, sculptors and painters came to the city. They took up residence directly next to the building site, erected their own small houses between the Zwinger, the building site and the Elbe. Thus arose the Italian village, the last remains of which disappeared in the middle of last century in connection with the new design of Theaterplatz. The name has remained, and it finally passed to the gastronomic building constructed by Hans Erlwein in 1911, which was restored in 1957 and reconstructed in 1992/1993.

From 1739 to 1756, the last great architectural work of Roman Baroque arose as a splendid symbol of the Catholic creed, which had regained a footing in Saxony. After fortifications had been demolished, the Hofkirche (court church) was built between the Augustusbrücke (Augustus Bridge) and the palace. For urban design reasons, the church could not be built to face eastwards. With a ground area of 4800 square metres, it is still the largest church in Saxony. The nave with the high altar, two side aisles, four corner chapels and the strictly separated, finely structured spire with a hight of 85.5 metres fully corresponded to the requirements of Catholic services. Catholic processions were not permitted in the open air in Protestant Saxony, so a two-storey procession passage was built between

the nave and the two side aisles. As the court church, enclosed boxes of honour were included on the gallery of the nave for the royal family, and they were connected to the palace by an overhead passage. 59 sandstone pictures created by Lorenzo Mattielli decorate the balustrades of the two storeys of the church. From 1750 to 1754, an organ was built for the church by the old master organ builder, Gottfried Silbermann and completed by his pupil Hildebrandt. This organ was taken into storage elsewhere during the Second World War and is the only Silbermann organ in Dresden that is still preserved. Like George Bähr in the Frauenkirche (Church of Our Lady), Chiaveri was also faced with severe criticism by those who claimed that the curvature of the nave would collapse. In 1746 the building work was discontinued for this reason, and in 1749 Chiaveri left Dresden, frustrated and bitter. It was only when the painter Anton Raphael Mengs climbed the dome with his father and declared it safe that construction was continued, under the leadership of Johann Christoph Knöffel until 1752, and was then under the leadership of the head state master builder, Julius Heinrich Schwarze. The church was consecrated on 29th June 1751 and completed in 1756, the year when the Seven Years War began. The church was heavily damaged by explosive bombs in 1945. Reconstruction work was begun soon after the end of the war, but it is still not completely finished. However, it has been possible to use the nave for church

services again since 1962. The church also became the burial place of the Albertine Wettins who had become Catholics. Four crypts contain 49 sarcophages, starting from Friedrich August II and his closest relatives. In a small silver capsule which is gilded on the inside, in accordance with his own wish, is the heart of August the Strong, whose body is buried in the cathedral on the Wavel in Krakow.

Taschenbergpalais (Taschenberg Palace)
Even those who have little knowledge of Saxon history have probably heard of the mistresses of the most famous Elector of Saxony and King of Poland, August the Strong. The Taschenbergpalais opposite the palace is a reminder of this reputation. As from 1995 it now presents itself as a comfortable hotel, the "best address in town".

The great conflict between the Russian Czar Peter the Great – allied with the Danish King Frederick IV and the Saxon Elector Friedrich August I, who was also the king of Poland – and the Swedish King Karl XII, who was actively supported by France and the Ottoman Empire, for political supremacy in the northern part of the European continent was in full swing when August the Strong suffered bitter defeats. In 1704, he practically lost the throne of Poland. His cousin from Sweden installed Stanislaw Leszczynski as the King of Poland, and August had to stay in Dresden. There on 7th December 1704, at the fire of the house of

Taschenbergpalais (Taschenberg Palace)

his general excise director, Adolph Magnus von Hoym, he got to know Hoym's wife, Anna Constantia, who had been born in the von Brockdorff family and came from the Holstein region. Months later, a new amorous adventure began for the Elector. Anna Constantia became his mistress for at least seven years and he gave her a promise of marriage even before she was divorced from Hoym. On 15th June 17054 August bought the Haugwitzsche house for her, which was situated near the palace on a small rise known as the Taschenberg. Six more citizens' plots of land were then purchased, and August had a palace built on them. Anna Constantia, who was given the name of Imperial Countess of Cosel by Emperor Joseph I in Vienna in 1706 after great effort on the part of August, and her royal lover had great influence on the architectural design, which is otherwise largely ascribed to the work of the head state master builder, Johann Friedrich Karcher. But Johann Christoph Naumann and Matthäus Daniel Pöppelmann also showed their masterful abilities in this palace. The Imperial countess held court there, and at the side of August she received kings and diplomats, ministers and privy councillors, and court festivals and celibrations were organised. When Countess Cosel fell into displeasure in 1713 and was finally condemned to life imprisonment in Stolpen Castle on Christmas Eve 1716, August the Strong confiscated her possessions. For the Taschenbergpalais,

which he refurnished after 1715, the Elector and king finally found a new use in 1718. In 1719 the palace, which represented a decisive step in the development of residential palace construction in Dresden, was allocated to the Electoral prince and his wife after reconstruction was carried out in 1718/1719 by Pöppelmann and Rayomnd Le Plat. On 2nd September 1719, August's legitimate son Friedrich August and his wife, Archduchess Maria Josepha, the daughter of Emperor Joseph I, ceremoniously entered Dresden and moved into the house. It remained the residence of the Electoral princes until the end of the monarchy. After 1945, only the facade of the Taschenbergpalais remained standing.

In the mid-1980s, the reconstruction plans prepared in the GDR period envisaged the construction of a general scientific library and a youth centre. Now, the building will again be used for a purpose which the house had from the time when it was first built – the reception and temporary accommodation of visitors from all parts of the world, including royal guests.

The old Landtag (state parliament) building – now the city museum
In Wilsdruffer Strasse shortly before it reaches Pirnaischer Platz, the place where the visitor leaves the old part of the city at the south, only one building from the 18th century is still preserved. Today, after its reconstruction from 1963 to 1966, it accom-

modates the museum of the city of Dresden. In sophisticated form with interesting exhibits spanning 800 years, the museum presents the changeable history of Dresden to its citizens and their visitors. This history also includes the fact that Dresden, as the residence of the Wettin rulers from 1631, was the permanent meeting place of the state parliament of the Electoral Saxon territory.

At a meeting of prelates, dukes, knights and towns convened in Leipzig in 1438 by the Saxon Elector Friedrich II, they persuaded the ruler of the state, in return for a levy of taxes, to grant them the right to meet for joint consultations without a special summons from the Elector. That was the birth of the Saxon state parliament, which represented the interests of society and was organised in terms of social ranks. In the 393 years of its existence (its last meeting was held in 1831), the state parliament indulged in state politics both for and against the ruler of the state, promoted general political developments, and at times hindered or even prevented them. The state parliament was made up of three curies. In the first curie, the prelates, dukes and lords met, the second curie was made up of the knights and the third was made up by the towns. The state parliament meetings began with a church service in the Sophenkirche (St. Sophie's Church), followed by joint consultations and separate consultations according to a fixed ceremonial procedure which was precisely defined

The old Landtag (state parliament)
building (now the City Museum)

by August the Strong in 1728 in a state parliament statute. At the opening of the state parliament, the social ranks gathered in the palace, where the state ruler had his proposition, his wishes and demands for the ranks read out to them. Then the curies convened for days or even weeks, and the second and third curies met separately in respective general sessions and smaller committees. They collated the "Gravamina", the complaints of the state, and argued about them until they reached a consensus, and then they presented this preliminary document, which also included the sanction by the ranks, to the ruler of the state. The state parliament, which usually met for several months, was finally closed by the ruler of the state in the state parliament closing ceremony.

For many centuries, the representatives of the ranks of the Electoral Saxon state had no building of their own in which to consult and work. They met in Dresden from 1631 and the conference rooms of the curies and committees were spread around the city centre. While the smaller committee of the knights met in the Kanzleihaus (chamber house) and the first curie and the wider meeting of the knights met in Schloßstrasse, the general meeting of the knights met in the old Gewandhaus and the towns met in Breite Gasse. The distance from the seat of the ruler of the state at the same time documented the differences between the ranks. It was only when the new Landhaus (state parliament building) was built from 1770 to 1776 by the Academy of Arts professor and head state master builder, Friedrich August Krubsacius, that the representatives of the ranks in the state acquired their own building. Their accommodation within the building corresponded to the concept of social rank: the smaller committee of knights met in the most splendid room in the centre of the building on the first floor, the first curie and the other committees of the second curie met in the side wings of the first floor, the third curie with its committees met on the second and third floor – and the third floor was only accessible via an auxiliary staircase. After Saxony became a constitutional monarchy in September 1831, the Landhaus became the meeting place of the conference of the ranks, which were separated into the First Chamber and Second Chamber, following the English parliamentary system. The representative body convened there until it was relocated to the house of the ranks which was erected at the beginning of the 20th century at Schlossplatz. Only once was there a brief interruption in the harmonious relationship between the Saxon king and the parliament. At the opening of the "Nonsensical parliament" elected in February 1849, the delegates did not go to the palace to hear the opening speech of the government in the presence of the monarch; instead, the monarch and ministers went to the delegates in the Landhaus.

Concerning the architecture as we see it today, it remains to be said that the master builder Krubsacius, a pupil of Longuelune, departed from Pöppelmann and his associates and attempted to allow a greater simplicity and rationality to take effect in the building. In the interior, however, there is one of the most beautiful staircases in Dresden, a staircase which is adorned with artistic wrought iron railings. Although the building has not changed its site, the beauty of the architecture of the building only became fully apparent after 1875 when Johannstrasse was cleared up to Pirnaischer Platz, thus making the courtyard side into the street side. The portal which originally completed the court side was removed in 1957. Now, this portal is the entrance to the Baroque gardens at Großsedlitz.

The "Balcony" of Europa

The Brühlsche Terrasse (Brühl Terrace)

From Schlossplatz, a generously constructed stairway with 41 low steps leads to the Brühlsche Terrasse. But this stairway has only existed since 1814 when it was built by Gottlieb Friedrich Thormeyer by the command of the Russian General Governor Count Repnin, who had been resident in the Brühlsche Palace since November 1813. Until then, access was only possible from the side facing the city and it annoyed the General Governor, who ruled the Kingdom of Saxony on behalf of the victorious allies, that he could not take a direct route from his residence to the palace. The construction of the open air stairway now permitted general access to this part of the city, which had been the private property of the Prime Minister Duke Heinrich von Brühl, who gave his name to a whole period of Saxon history. Now the citizens could walk in Brühl's garden, which after Brühl's death again came into the possession of the Elector/king and was repaired, and they could watch the busy activities on the Elbe and enjoy the view of the Elbe valley which was wider here, but came closer to the river again further upstream and downstream. Soon, the Brühlsche Terrasse was given the name "Balcony of Europe", a unique municipal complex which no other European city can rival. When the visitor has climbed the stairway, at the foot of which there were once two stylised lions created by the sculptor Christian Gottlieb Kühne and today

situated in the Grosser Garten, he first has a beautiful view of the Hofkirche (court church), the Georgenbau (Georg building) of the palace and the Schlossplatz, and also of the Italian village and the Augustusbrücke (Augustus Bridge). To the right and left of the open air stairway there are four groups of figures created by one of the major sculptors of the 19th century in Dresden, Johannes Schilling. They represent the four times of day. Originally made of sandstone, they were covered in gold in 1883, and in 1903, because of the danger of weathering, they were cast in bronze. The bronze casts are now in Dresden in place of the originals, and the originals are in Chemnitz.

Unfortunately, nothing is left of the buildings which Brühl had built from 1737 onwards on the fortification embankment which had been built by Elector Moritz. The present buildings are all the result of structural alterations in the second half of the 19th century. The first great building project which changed the face of the Brühlsche Terrasse was the work on the armoury from 1884 to 1887 to convert it into the main state archive and a building for the sculpture collection, now known as the Albertinum. The monumental main front does not show itself to its full effect because it is hidden by a park complex on which Brühl's Belvedere stood. Directly afterwards from 1891 onwards, Konstantin Lipsius, the successor of Nicolai at the Academy, con-

The Brühlsche Terrasse
(Brühl Terrace)

Monument to Ernst Rietschel

41

structed the ostentatious building for the Academy of the Arts, the training institution founded in 1764 for painters, sculptors and architects at which outstanding specialists in their respective areas taught in the 19th and 20th century, and from which students graduated who later became outstanding artists. Next to it, the building of the Saxon Art Association was erected in the same style of Dresden historicism with its over-proportioned glass dome, known locally as the lemon press, and above it the figure of the nix, which is a marked structure in the silhouette of the old city of Dresden. When the dome of Bähr's Frauenkirche (Church of Our Lady) was still standing, this new dome structure was felt to be disturbing. "What disturbs is the miserable glass dome next to the monumental dome of Bähr's Frauenkirche," wrote an art historian at the beginning of the 20th century. When the Frauenkirche has been rebuilt, it will be seen whether this is still true 100 years later. The building between the Academy of the Arts and the state parliament building is most in keeping with th original character of the Brühlsche Terrasse because this building, known as "Sekundogenitur", was built in place of Brühl's library in a neo-Baroque style. The successors sold the 62,000 volumes of the Brühlsche library to the Electoral library. Until 1931, the new building accommodated the library and copper engraving collection of the second-born Albertine Wettins up to 1918.

Since its reconstruction in the 1960s, the "Sekundogenitur" has been used as a gastronomy complex. In good weather, the guest can sit on the Brühlsche Terrasse, drink coffee and eat ice-cream. This deliberately continues the tradition which developed from the time when the gardens on the fortification embankment were first opened – going for a stroll, being seen and then sitting down to coffee, cakes and ice-cream, gossipping and discussing. The Belvedere, which Knöffel built for Brühl in 1747 was demolished in 1759 at the command of Friedrich the Great, rebuilt by Schuricht in 1814 and finally demolished and replaced by a new building by Otto von Wolframsdorf in 1842. In this building was the renowned Café reale of the Italian, Enrico Torniamenti. Its guests included Semper and Rietschel, Schumannn and Wagner, and it was the birthplace of the "Hiller coffee group" from which the famous "Monday society" arose in 1846. Around 1830, an anonymous visitor to the city described the Brühlsche Terrasse with the words: "A different attractiveness of prospect awaits you here; here, not even our delegates and ministers disdain to sit, and the evening walk which extends along this charming embankment is hardly equalled anywhere. It presses the beauty of the ladies together in a small space; people know each other and are greeted and swept away, and there is much to see and feel at each step. The small park to the side is exquisite; it is

our Tuileries, our Pincio, our Púerta del Sol, the resting bench and Belvedere of every stranger and traveller."

Monument to Ernst Rietschel
After 1831, the Dresden Academy of the Arts was systematically staffed with young and gifted teachers, which was particularly due to the liberal state minister, Bernhard August von Lindenau and the co-regent and later king, Friedrich August II. In the 1830s and 1840s, the Academy developed to become a centre of German painting and architecture. In 1832, the 28-year old sculptor Ernst Rietschel, who was born in 1804 in Pulsnitz and had trained in Berlin under the famous Rauch, was called to Dresden as a professor. In 1834 the 31-year old Gottfried Semper, born in 1803 in Altona, was appointed to the post of professor of architecture, which had been vacant since 1833. In 1838, on a recommendation from Semper, the 27-year old Ernst Julius Hähnel, who was born in Dresden, returned to Dresden from Munich. Rietschel and Hähnel founded the Dresden school of sculpture of the 19th century, and together with Semper they created immortal buildings in Dresden – the master builder creating the buildings in the Renaissance style, the two sculptors adding the decorative sculptures on the Semper Gallery and Semper Opera House. There were also the painters Ludwig Richter, Carl Christian Vogel von Vogelstein, Julius Hübner and Eduard Bendemann. It was a group about

which the young Munich painter and writter Friedrich Pecht wrote in 1836: "For Richter had an unusually independent spirit … But he only showed his delightful humour in a whisper in a small group when he quietly sat together in the café with Öhme and Peschel, the most intimate friends of his youth, so that this group was soon christened as "the three kings". But Rietschel, who was a strange mixture of a volcano and a poor village teacher both in his appearance and in his character, with all his ingrained humility still had all the fire and insatiability of a genious, and it was not for no reason that he married four women one after the other. With these two men and the recently appointed Semper, a completely new artistic life was predestined for Dresden. Each of them bore a new world within his breast, as was soon to be revealed."

The Dresden public honoured the work of a man who had created unique monuments by creating a monument for him. His pupil Johannes Schilling designed the monument in 1876, and it was cast in the Einsiedeln foundry in Lauchhammer. It was erected in a position on the Brühlsche Terrasse which had become free after the demolition of a building in 1872 and which was directly connected with the person thus honoured. Rietschel's monument was erected at the former site of the Brühlsche garden room in which his school of industry was housed in 1814, which marked the starting point for the foundation of the Techni-

cal Training Institution in 1828 which was initially also accommodated there. Lohrmann opened the new teaching institution there, the fourth of its kind in the German League. In 1833, Rietschel set up his atelier in this garden room.

A trip on the Elbe by steamship

There is no better way to enjoy the beautiful scenery on both sides of the upper Elbe between Diesbar to the north of Meissen and Schmilka on the Saxon-Bohemian border than on board a paddle steamship belonging to the "Weisse Flotte" (White Fleet) boating company. Castles and palaces pass by as if on a string of pearls, vineyards delight the eye on the south-facing slopes of the Elbe valley from Diesbar-Seussnitz via the Bosel, the Spaargebirge hills and Hoflössnitz to Pillnitz, wooded heights and the uniquely shaped rocks of the Elbsandsteingebirge greet the steamship with an intimacy that equals the towns and villages. The steamer glides along gracefully with its huge paddle wheels to port and starboard which move smoothly and evenly through the water, powered by the shining pistons of a steam engine. If it were not for the railway bridges and the road bridges with their never-ending processions of vehicles crossing the Elbe and the industrial complexes from Coswig to Heidenau and Pirna – albeit with less significance in recent years – the traveller could imagine himself transported into the second half of the 19th century.

A good 160 years ago, Dresden merchants got together to provide the same experience in this German model area of the industrial revolution that travelling Saxons had experienced on rivers in North America: a trip on a river with a ship propelled by a steam engine and not by wind or by human muscle power like the "Bomätscher" boats on the Elbe. The Dresden merchants were not only motivated by the reputation of participating in technical progress, they were also attracted by the prospect of making a good profit by providing convenient, cheap and, above all, faster transport between Hamburg, Dresden and Bohemia. In order to implement such a project in Dresden, they needed a royal privilege. This was finally granted in 1836 after extensive negotiations.

The "Comité der Elbdampfschiffahrts-Gesellschaft" (Committee of the Elbe Steamship Company) commissioned Johann Andreas Schubert to build the ships. Schubert was born in 1808 and was Professor of Engineering at the Technical training institution which had been founded in 1827 as the fifth institution of its kind in Europe. In that year, together with Wilhelm Gotthelf Lohrmann, he had founded the "Dresdner Actien-Maschinenbau-Verein" (Dresden shareholding engineering association), and he had set up an engineering workshop in Übigau. The first two passenger steamships on the Elbe were built there. For one ship Schubert designed and built an iron hull,

Dresden in the evening

A trip on the Elbe by steamship

The "Basteischlösschen" (Bastei Palace –
water level indicator) on the terrace bank

47

the other ship had a wooden hull. Both ships were fitted with low pressure steam engines. On 30th July 1837, the "Königin Maria" sailed from Übigau and put to shore below the Augustusbrücke (Augustus Bridge) in Dresden. The initiators of the construction of the ships, the designers with their families and the invited guests of honour boarded the ship and went on the first trip, which was a great success. In one and a half hours they were in Meissen, which at that time was an incredibly short time for the journey. The return journey upstream naturally took longer.

The first public trip on the "Königin Maria" from Dresden to Rathen took place on 11th August 1837. That was the beginning of pleasure trips on the Elbe. A contemporary wrote: "That was a major event for Dresden … when the first steamships sailed on our Elbe. The majority of the populace had never even seen a steamship and had hardly any idea of the power of steam. … When regular trips on the Upper Elbe began, Pillnitz came very much into its own. Not only on Sundays; trips there were also made on weekdays."

But the steamships did not only sail for the pleasure of the citizens and the transportation of goods. On the afternoon of 3rd May 1849, the armed battle for the acceptance of the Imperial constitution had begun in Dresden. Under the impression of the first barricades, the general uprising of the citizens and the lack of military resis-

tance, King Friedrich August II, the entire royal family and all the ministers left the city at about three o'clock in the early morning of 4th May to escape to the Königstein. The later King Johann wrote in his memoirs: "In the early morning they then left the palace and went across the bridge on foot. On the right bank of the Elbe, a steamship was to be held ready near the pontoon shed. There was a dense fog and considerable fear when the ship requested was not found. … Finally the ship was discovered and the embarcation and the journey were completely happy…"

Steamship travel on the Elbe developed rapidly. In 1857 a purpose-built shipyard was constructed in Blasewitz, and in 1898 it was relocated to Laubegast. On 26th March 1867, the Dresden company was changed to "Sächsisch-Böhmische Dampfschiffahrts-Gesellschaft" (Saxon-Bohemian Steamship Company). In 1897 the company had 20 paddle steamers, and in 1911 this number had grown to 33. The last paddle steamer, the "Leipzig", was taken into commission in 1929. Only eleven ships of this fleet with worldwide significance survived the year 1945. Many steamers from the fleet burned at the terrace banks, were taken to the USSR as compensation payment or were confiscated by the Czechs. Only gradually was the rest of the "Weisse Flotte" freed from its camouflage paint and converted back from hospital ships to passenger ships. In addition to the paddle steamers which were still

perserved, seven motor ships were added in the 1960s, 1970s and 1980s. Where the ships of the Saxon-Bohemian Steamship Company transported a total of 3.5 million passengers in 1898, in the GDR period there were still as many as 1.5 million passengers. In 1995 there were 605,000 passengers who travelled on the Elbe in the ten ships of the company which was privatised in 1992. They used the paddle steamers "Rathen", "Leipzig" (taken into service in 1929), "Pillnitz", "Dresden", "Pirna", "Diesbar", "Meissen" and "Wehlen" (taken into service in 1879) and the motor saloon ships "August the Strong" and "Countess Cosel". With this fleet of ships, the Saxon steamship company, in which the Free State of Saxony has a holding of 51 per cent, is the oldest and largest paddle steamer fleet in the world.

The "Basteischlösschen" (Bastei Palace) on the terrace bank

The city and its residents have always had to live with the Elbe, with floods and low water. When the snow masses on the Riesengebirge, the Isergebirge and the Erzgebirge suddenly melted in the spring, there was usually a spring flood in Dresden. But summer and winter floods were also not unknown. And if there was a hot dry summer, the water level of the Elbe often fell below normal. But in all seasons and every day, shipping on the Elbe was dependent on the Elbe water level. Therefore, regular water level measurements became a necessity in the 19th century. The first water level indicator at the Augustusbrücke (Augustus Bridge) was fitted by the mineralogist and chronicler of Saxon Elbe flooding, Christian Gottlieb Poetzsch, in about 1800. Wilhelm Gotthelf Lohrmann, the important geodesist, topographer, meteorologist and cofounder of the Technical Training Institution continued these observations and surveyed the Elbe from 1820 onwards. As a result of his measurements, the Elbe river map was published in 1828. On 73 sectional sheets, the course of the Elbe and its bed, including the bank zones, were surveyed and cartographed from the Prussian border to the Bohemian border. Saxony had thus fulfilled an important condition of the Elbe Shipping Act of 1822 and the conferences that had been held.

Between the survey of the Elbe by Lohrmann and a technical correction of the Elbe course which subsequently took place, thus accelerating the flow of the water, the river bed deepened by about 90 centimetres in a little over half a century. That gave the occasion to redefine the zero point of the Dresden level indicator in 1934. With effect from 1st January 1935 it was fixed at 103 metres above mean sea level, and a new measuring scale was attached to the first bridge support of the Augustusbrücke on the old city side. The water level registration and recording office of the Saxon waterways office is accommodated in a small building nearby which is situated on the wall of the old

Dresden embankment complex. It is the so-called "Basteischlösschen". In connection with the construction of the Italian village by Hans Erlwein, the stylistically related, single-storey "Basteischlösschen" was built on the basis of a design by his staff member Carl Hirschmann. On the side facing the Elbe, a board is visible to all citizens which shows the daily level of the Dresden water indicator scale.

Because of the deepening of the bed of the Elbe, extreme high water levels such as the floods of 31st March 1845 with 6.30 metres and of 1890, which gave the impulse for extensive building work in the city, cannot be expected to be repeated as far as can be judged. The spring flood of 31st March 1845 produced the highest water level which has ever been recorded for the Elbe. A contemporary wrote in his diary: " A day which Dresden will not forget. During the night, the water swelled up to a height never seen before. The whole market in the Neustadt was almost completely covered. People travelled in boats on Klostergasse and Meissner Gasse. After ten o'clock, the column on which the crucifix stood suddenly came loose and the latter, together with the railing and pavement flew in a great arc into the water and a great column of water splashed up. … The Antonstadt is completely under water and there is said to be great distress on the surrounding land. If this lasts for several days, such distress will also be known here because nothing will be able to come in

from the land." The crucifix was not found again. At a water level of 4.70 metres, shipping is stopped now because it is no longer possible to pass the bridges, at a level of 5.30 metres the water covers the terrace bank.

On Theaterplatz

The Zwinger

In 1987, which was the 325th anniversary of the birth of Matthäus Daniel Pöppelmann and the 250th anniversary of his death, Dresden honoured the life's work of this great architect and master builder of the Baroque in Electoral Saxony with a major art exhibition and a number of scientific events. The associated publications yet again show that the Zwinger is an important feature of European architectural and artistic history. It is literally a symbol of the Augustine age, an expression in stone of the political claim of the Electors to play a wider role in the Holy Roman Empire of the German Nation of the 18th century than merely to govern the Albertine Electorate of Saxony. The people of Dresden and their visitors now regard the life's work of Pöppelmann and Permoser, with its three wings and the Semper Paintings Gallery completing the great court on the Theaterplatz side, as a building that is pleasing to the eye and that could not be created today in view of modern rational architectural styles. But when it was designed and built, it was part of the political will of an enlightened monarch who ruled in a very absolute manner.

Festivals and celebrations were a regular element of home and foreign policy at the court of August the Great. Some contemporaries described such events in far greater detail than the events of politics. The pleasures of the ruler of the state and his court included ballet performances of Italian and French comedies, court balls, festival banquets and costume balls, dissipated carnival events, so-called great entertainments, sledge rides, hunting, ring races and shooting contests. Apart from the court, the entire residence city and the surrounding area took a more or less lively interest in these events. The inhabitants of the city and the countryside were participants, court suppliers and wage earners who met the extensive orders of the court for such events in blossoming manufacturing companies and crafts enterprises. In some cases, the festivals and celebrations were thoroughly prepared for months in advance, and this was always under the clear personal direction of August the Strong. Under his rule, the festivals in Dresden and Warsaw were highlights of Baroque festival culture, and at the same time they were also an important element of Augustine government politics. That was shown in the important political events in electoral Saxony and in Europe. The most outstanding celebrations were the festivals in 1695 and 1697 for the coronation of Friedrich August I as the King of Poland, in 1709 on the occasion of the visit of King Frederick IV of Denmark to Dresden, in 1719 for the wedding of Electoral Prince Friedrich August to Maria Josepha von Habsburg, the daughter of Emperor Joseph I, in 1727 after August the Strong recovered from illness, in 1728 on the occasion of the visit of King Friedrich Wilhelm of Prussia and in 1730 in connection with Zeithain Camp.

Here, the general impression must be corrected that the Wettin ruler indulged in expensive court feasts because of his defeats in the Northern War. It was only when the defeat of Charles XII of Sweden in the Ukraine became known that August celebrated together with Frederick IV of Denmark from 22nd May to 2nd July 1709. It is certain that the ladies' festival, the fireworks organised by Pöppelmann, the foot contest, the four continents carousel, the procession of the gods with the night ring and quinte race, the farmers' restaurant with eight nations, the bird shooting and night shooting were only the outer framework for the serious political negotiations about the further procedure against Sweden. The situation was similar for the visits of Czar Peter I to Dresden in 1711 and 1712 and the visit of the Prussian king to Leipzig in 1710.

The celebrations in 1719 were a highlight of courtly Baroque festifities which was not repeated during the reign of August the Strong. At the beginning of the year, true to etiquette, the death of Charles XII of Sweden was mourned in Dresden with an official chamber mourning event, even though there was certainly relief at the passing of one of the most stubborn political opponents. A few months later was the celebration of the wedding of Electoral Prince Friedrich August with Maria Josepha von Habsburg, which was a political event of European significance because, with this

marriage, the Wettin dynasty rose to the closer circle of possible heirs to the Imperial throne. For August the Strong, that was a far more important reason for festivities. From 2nd to 26th September, one of the largest courtly festivals was held under his personal direction. Nothing shows the link between the struggle for power in foreign policy, the inner stability of the absolutely ruled Saxon state and its economic strength as clearly as the seven planet entertainments which were completed on the evening of 26th September with the "Berghäuer Fest" in the Plauen valley area.

It was natural, in view of the political and social importance that was associated with these festivals and celebrations, that a high artistic standard was aimed for. Therefore, all the available artists were called together for such festivals – architects, painters, musicians, minstrels, dancers, poets, sculptors, goldsmiths and silversmiths. Pöppelmann built pleasure houses and pleasure boats for fireworks in 1709 and 1730, the buildings and tents for the Zeithain Camp in 1730 and, of course, the Zwinger in Dresden as the special architectural setting for all celebrations. Balthasar, Permoser, Alessandro Mauro, Louis de Silvestre, Johann Jakob Irminger, Johann Melchior Dinglinger, Johann Ullrich König, Jean de Bodt, Adam Friedrich Zürner, Alexandere Thiele, Benjamin Thomae and many other artists with their creativity, ideas and works in the courtly festivals made a major contribution

to the status of Dresden in the first third of the 18th century as a residence city of European significance.

The starting point for the construction of the Zwinger was the wish of the young Elector Friedrich August I to redesign an unused part of the embankment complex to the west of the palace. In 1711, the idea arose of creating a terraced complex with arched galleries, and later the idea of adding pavilions on the embankment. The wooden amphitheatre was later converted to a stone structure. The complex was dominated by three pavilions: the bell tower with a bell chime made of Meissen porcelain which was only completed after 1722, the crown gate with the Polish throne watched over by two eagles, which was constructed between 1714 and 1718, and the embankment pavilion to crown the work in a uniquely successful combination of architecture and sculpture, which was built from 1716 to 1718. Arched galleries linked the pavilions, so that a great festive court was created measuring 204 metres in length and 116 metres in width. The side facing the Elbe remained open because building work was discontinued in 1738. It was only 100 years later that Gottfried Semper set about the task of closing this gap.

The motifs for the vivid decorative work were taken from the mythology of antiquity, which was at that time still generally known, and the intent of the work was dictated by the state ruler, the owner of the building, with the political targets that were already

A figure in the Nymphenbad
(Bathing of the nymphs)

The joys of winter in front of the Zwinger

The Wallpavillon (Embankment near
the Zwinger Pond Pavilion)

achieved or were still to be striven for. Flora, Ceres, Bacchus, Vulcan, Jupiter, Neptune, Apollo, herms and satyrs alternated with Electoral Saxon coats of arms, the Polish crown and the crown of the Empire. The combined artistic and architectural composition culminated in the embankment pavilion. There is no better description than that given in 1909 by Paul Schümann: "On the embankment pavilion, all of Mount Olymp congregates to witness the royal glory of August. The whole wealth of decorative splendour comes together here: strong and richly adorned herms rise from the ground to support the entabulature; the satyrs with their pointed ears, which bear the entabulature with their hands and heads, bend and press themselves against the weight, exerting their muscle power; exhaustion and effort or lust and drunkenness speak from their features, and some bite their arms and lips with anger. The task of bearing the weight is illustrated here in bold and crude sensuality. Rich cartouches decorate the end stones of the arches between the pillars, the outcrops of the ledges are crowned with vases containing luxuriant bouquets of fruit and flowers. With great delicacy the main motifs of the architecture are blended to ever changing forms and ornamentally underlined. The upper floor starts in a calmer fashion, with high arches between the pillars and, above the main ledge, the vivid ornamentation rising as a living symbol of free completion in festive splendour. The centre, surrounded by a majestically set cartouche of flowers, is the Polish and Saxon coat of arms. Leaning on it and blowing horns, fauna and their entourage can be seen in exciting movement, with the royal crown which August gained as the Electoral hat resting on the cushion at the top. At the side are the Olympic figures of Aphrodite and Paris, Pallas Athene and Artemis, Zeus and Hera, Aiolos the god of the wind, Iris, Hebe and Chloris, with a host of busy cherubs in between. On the massive central gable, which towers even higher than the attic roof, is Atlas who is strenuously bearing the world on his shoulders." He represents the Hercules of Saxony, "Hercules Saxonicus", whoe is repeatedly used as a motif both on the building and on coins and medals. He symbolises August of Saxony bearing the weight of his two countries.

Between the Wallpavillon (embankment pavilion) and the French pavilion is the Nymphenbad (nymphs' bath), an architectural gem of the Zwinger. It was also created in 1711, and with its enchanting water jets, the cascade, the large oyster shells and the water-spouting dolphins it represents an oasis of peace in the midst of the noisy city.

After the glorious times in the first half of the 18th century, there came a period which was at times unpleasant for this beautiful building. In the Seven Years War it was heavily damaged and used as a wood stacking and carpentry area. In the razing of the fortifications after 1810, the Zwinger moat was filled in. In May 1849, the Zwinger was again damaged by the fire in the opera house. After such disasters, attempts were always made to restore the building, for example in 1783, from 1852 to 1863 and from 1880 to 1898, but because of the use of cement, iron braces and oil paints these attempts caused more damage than preservation. It was only the fourth repair carried out under Hubert Ermisch from 1924 to 1936 which brought a significant improvement. In 1929, the Zwinger moat was dug out again, the old fortress walls were uncovered and the wooden bridge across the moat was constructed true to the historical model. But the Zwinger had hardly been restored to its former glory when it was completely destroyed in February 1945. Rebuilding work began in the summer of 1945, and in 1964 it was completed with the reconstruction of the Wallpavillon. In the course of this building work, the Zwinger moat was connected to the Zwinger pond which had been ceated in 1820. As a result, a unique small park was created in the centre of the city which offers relaxation and recreation after a strenuous tour of the city or a visit to a museum. When a hard winter causes the moat and pond to freeze over, which does not often happen in the course of a century, the people of Dresden take possession of the ice surface.

After more than thirty years, however, the time has now come for the next and most extensive repairs to the Zwinger.

Semper Gallery and Schinkelwache
(Schinkel Guard House)

59

Semper Gallery and Schinkelwache (Schinkel Guard House)

If the visitor proceeds from the Taschenbergpalais towards Theaterplatz, he then stands in front of a building which does not really fit the architectural situation. To the right is the palace built in the Renaissance style and the Baroque Hofkirche (court church), to the left the painting gallery Alte Meister (Old Masters) by Gottfried Semper in the style of the Italian Renaissance, and in the background Semper's court opera building in the style of the High Renaissance. The building concerned is the only one in the Berlin Classical style to be built in Dresden. Karl Friedrich Schinkel had designed the old city guard house, and it was built from 1830 to 1832 under Professor Joseph Thürmer, who was appointed to the Academy of the Arts in 1827 and died very early. Even the Saxonia figure seated on a lion and the Saxon coat of arms do not make the building more Saxonian in its appearance.

When Thürmer died suddenly and unexpectedly in 1833, an attempt was made to call Karl Friedrich Schinkel to Dresden, but the Prussian head state director of buildings refused and suggested a pupil of his instead. An offer made by the Saxon government to the well-known architect Franz Christian Gau, who was working in Paris, met with a similar reaction; Gau then suggested Semper. The decision was then made in favour of this young architect. As a result, construc-

tion in Dresden until 1849 was dominated by Semper, and then by his pupils. Besides the opera house, the best known work of Semper in the old part of the city is the painting gallery, which was begun in 1847. Not even the shell of the "Neues Museum" was finished when the democratically minded professor, who had had barricades built in Dresden to professional standards against his government, had to escape from the city on 9th May 1849 and went into exile. From 11th June 1849, the Saxon police searched for him throughout the whole of Europe with an arrest warrant. An autocratic legal pronouncement by King Johann in July 1863 was necessary to settle in Semper's favour his troublesome nationality dispute and the resulting military service obligation for his four sons. After Semper's flight, the painting gallery was continued by Krüger and Haenel and completed in 1854. Semper brilliantly completed Pöppelmann's Zwinger on the Elbe side facing Theaterplatz.

Looking towards the Semper Opera House

Next to the Zwinger with the crown gate, the Semper Opera House, which was rebuilt from 1977 to 1985, has become a hallmark of Dresden. Since the reopening of what is now the third Semper Opera House with the performance of the "Freischütz" (Freeshooter) by Carl Maria von Weber, the opera house has almost always been sold out, whether the performance was an opera, a concert or a ballet. Those do not have a

subscription, advance booking ticket or hotel reservation will perhaps try to obtain a ticket in the evening outside the gates of the opera house or to buy a returned ticket. Not only the inside of the opera house is attractive, with its entrance hall, foyers, auditorium, curtain and 5-minute clock over the stage – the opera cast and the musicians of the state orchestra, with their outstanding artistic performances, form a union with the architectural setting.

From the 17th century, when the court music director Heinrich Schütz had his first German opera performance, "Daphne", staged in Torgau, opera performances formed part of cultural court life in Dresden. When Italian opera became established in Dresden during the reign of Elector Johann Georg II, the idea of a separate opera house soon arose. From 1664 to 1667, Wolf Caspar von Klengel built the Opera House at the Taschenberg, which was used until 1707. Then, Matthäus Daniel Pöppelmann built the opera house at the Zwinger in 1718/1719, which was converted to a ballroom in 1782. The only theatre in Dresden that could be used for performances was then the Comedy House in the Italian village, which was built in 1755. When Semper was called to Dresden in 1834 the Comedy House, which held an audience of 800, was inadequate and dilapidated, and the idea of reopening the Opera House at the Zwinger was repeatedly met with misgivings. The young and energetic architect took up the

The Semper Opera House

unsolved problem, drafted a number of plans for a new design of the area between the Zwinger, the Catholic Hofkirche (court church) and the bank of the Elbe, and suggested a new theatre building in this area. Again and again he mentioned this Zwinger Forum. Finally, in April 1838, the decision was made in the council of ministers in the presence of the king that Dresden would be provided with a new court theatre. In the same year, construction began in the style of the Italian Renaissance. The first performance was on 12th April 1841 with Schiller's "Torquato Tasso". The play was seen by an audience of 1750. Most of the sculptors and painters employed by the Academy of the Arts were involved in the artistic adornment of the court theatre and others came to Dresden especially for the purpose: Ernst Rietschel, Ernst Julius Hähnel, Julius Hübner, Edouard Désiré, Josef Despléchin, Jules Michel Diéterle and Charles Sédan. This first court theatre by Semper became the scene of the work of Carl Reissinger, Richard Wagner, August Röckel, Wilhelmine Schröder-Devrient, Josef Tichatschek, Eduard Devrient and many other musicians and singers.

This wonderful opera house, which saw the first performances of operas by Wagner, splendid performances of operas by Mozart and symphonies by Beethoven, was consumed by flames on the afternoon of 21st September 1869. While laying gas pipes over the chandelier, one of the two fitter's assistants lit a match and started a fire which the fire brigade was not able to extinguish. After the fire, only the outer walls were left standing. As early as 8th December 1869, King Johann issued a decree to the ranks in which he announced the reconstruction of the opera house and requested that an advance on the building costs should be granted from the state budget because the royal family was not able to finance the reconstruction on its own. He also announced an architects' competition in which Gottfried Semper, who had lived in Zurich as a Swiss citizen since 1861, was also to be invited to participate. After long and controversial debates and public discussion, especially in the press, the second chamber of the Saxon parliament resolved on 22nd February 1870 to grant the financial subsidy, to place the reconstruction in the hands of Gottfried Semper and to retain the previous site. Thus, construction work on the second Semper opera building in Dresden began with the laying of the foundation stone on 26th April 1871 under the direction of Semper's son, Manfred Semper. The building was formally opened on 2nd February 1878 with Goethe's "Iphigenie auf Tauris". For almost three quarters of a century whis building, which fully met the contemporary principles of theatre construction, was a major centre of theatrical art in Europe. This was especially the result of the work of Ernst von Schuck, who was a member of the opera and the state orchestra from 1872 until his death on 10th May 1914 and their director from 1882. Under his influence, Dresden became a "dorado for first performances", especially of the operas of Richard Strauss and Giacomo Puccini. The second Semper opera house again burned down, this time on 13th/14th February 1945. Again, only the outer walls were left standing. After reinforcement

work in the 1950s, there were repeated efforts by the people of Dresden to rebuild the opera house. But this desire and dream of fans of the Dresden opera throughout the world was only fulfilled over 30 years after destruction; the third Semper opera house in Dresden was constructed, and again it fulfilled the new requirements of stage and theatrical technology.

On the middle of Theaterplatz is a statue of a rider. This monument could not have had a better setting than outside the opera house because it is a statue of the Wettin ruler under whose reign the construction of the second Semper court theatre began: King Johann of Saxony. The monument, which is the work of Johannes Schilling, was unveiled on the occasion of the 800th anniversary of Wettin rule on 19th June 1889. It honours a Saxon ruler who had a knowledge and education which was hardly rivalled by anyone of his time. Under the pseudonym of "Philateles", the friend of truth, he published a valid German translation of Dante's "Divine Comedy" between 1833 and

1848, thus securing for himself a respected place in German literary history. During his reign, which began in 1854 after the fatal accident of his brother in Tirol, he was faced with difficult decisions. In 1866 he aligned with Austria in the German League, and after the military defeat against Prussia near Königrätz, he had to enter the Prussian-dominated North German League and then the Wilhelmine Empire, which was certainly not easy for him.

The new Saxon Landtag (state parliament) building

The official ceremony held by the Free State of Saxony to celebrate the third anniversary of its accession to the Federal Republic of Germany was held on 3rd October 1993 in the newly built assembly room of the Saxon state parliament. Thus, after two years of construction work, the third parliamentary building constructed in Dresden for the elected delegates to the Saxonian parliament was taken into use. It was also the first newly constructed state building after the renewed proclamation of the Free State of Saxony on the Albrechtsburg in Meissen on 3rd October 1990. Thus, the provisional accommodation of the state parliament in the Dreikönigskirche (Church of the Three Kings) during its first term of office, which became necessary on 27th October 1990, came to an end.

With the beginning of the second term of office, 120 members moved into the assembly room. The modern structure of glass and steel fits harmoniously into the architectural ensemble on the left bank of the Elbe between the Brühlsche Terrasse and the Marienbrücke bridge. The building was designed by Peter Kulka, an architect who was born in Dresden and now lives in Cologne, and it represents modern architecture at the end of the 20th century and does not need to shrink from a comparison with the two neighbouring buildings, which were also representative of their time: the second opera building by Gottfried Semper and the storehouse designed in 1912/1913 by Hans Erlwein. The end wall of the assembly room, which is extremely practically furnished for parliamentary work, is decorated by a sty- lised map of the Free State of Saxony in the borders of 3rd October 1990. This also gives expression to the new start of Saxony as a federal state, after the states had been abo- lished in the GDR in August 1952. The state has now become larger than it was in 1945 and 1952.

With the signature of King Friedrich August I under the peace treaty with Prussia and Russia on 18th May 1815 in Pressburg, the area of Saxony was reduced by about two thirds of its area. The forfeited territories, which stretched from Bober and Queis in the east to the Werra river in the west, were allocated to Prussia. Saxony retained a total area of 14,992.94 square kilometres. When the Prussian state was dissolved by the Allies in 1946, the Prussian area of Oberlausitz,

with Görlitz as its centre, was returned to Saxony. The same happened in the autumn of 1990 when, after referendums in the re- spective areas, the inhabitants of the districts of Eilenburg, Torgau, Delitzsch, Hoyers- werda and Weisswasser decided to belong to the Free State of Saxony. The area of Saxony today is about 18,000 square kilometres with about four and a half million inhabitants who are represented by the 120 members of the Saxon state parliament in Dresden. This representation now takes place in a building of which the state parliament president Er- ich Iltgen wrote in 1993: "The new assembly room surrounded with glass gives both a view of the inside and a view of the outside. Its design is also a symbol of the will of the Saxon parliament to make its decisions open and transparent for every citizen of our state."

After a fundamental decision by the state parliament and the state government at the beginning of 1991 that the Saxon state par- liament would have its permanent site on the land of the state financial directorate er- ected in the Weimar Republic, the assembly room and the alterations to the building which already existed represented the third parliamentary building project in the Saxon state capital. In 1991 that meant that the parliament deliberately decided not to use the parliamentary buliding built in Augu- stusstrasse from 1901 to 1907 by Paul Wallot, the architect of the Reichstag building in Berlin.

In the new Saxon Landtag
(state parliament) building

The Ministry of Finance

In the last third of the 19th century, the kingdom of Saxony and its state capital, Dresden, saw a veritable building boom. There were many reasons for this. The so-called foundation years were not without their effect on Saxony, which was forced to join the North German League in 1866 and the German Empire in 1871 after losing the battle of Königgrätz. Economic development, the beginning of new branches of industry, an explosive growth in the population with an unprecedented spread of the cities even beyond the mediaeval city walls, most of which fell in the first third of the 19th century, were typical of the situation in Saxony. This not only applied to Dresden but also to Chemnitz, Plauen, Zwickau and, of course, Leipzig. Within just a few decades, new residential areas arose before the turn of the century on land that belonged to incorporated suburbs. New bridges, an ever more dense railway network, which was especially concentrated at the junctions of Leipzig and Dresden, horse tracks, numerous new public buildings and private residential and business buildings sprang up. Stations and post offices, schools and town halls, court and administrative buildings were built in the towns and villages. The quantity and variety of building tasks surpassed the resources of individual architects. Thus, architectural offices arose which put the individual architect and his ideas in the background and only put the name of the office

on the facade. Lossow, Kühne and Viehweger were the leading architectural firms which dominated the style of the era with their important buildings. State building projects were financed by the greatly increased tax revenue amounting to millions.

The strands of the economic, financial and political development came together in the capital city of Saxony. Soon, the buildings dating from the 16th and 18th centuries which had housed the Saxon ministries since their constitution in the great state reform in 1831/1835 were no longer sufficient. Thus, new buildings were constructed for the central administrative authorities in Dresden. In defiance of established urban planning principles, two massive ministerial buildings were successively constructed on the Neustadt bank of the Elbe, the Ministry of Finance and the general ministerial building. They are still standing today, and after a gap of 50 years they again accommodate the State Chancellery and the ministries of the Free State of Saxony, thus regaining their original function. They also form the basis and the starting point for the development of a government district in Dresden, which has not so far existed.

The first of these ministerial buildings was the Ministry of Finance, built on land which belonged to the treasury. The houses and installations of the Saxon army which had been there for decades became useless in 1880 when the XII (Saxon) army corps acquired new accommodation in the north

of Dresden on the edge of Dresden Heath. The area which thus became vacant in the Neustadt (new part of the city) was ideal for building. In place of the low pontoon sheds, the new Ministry of Finance building was constructed from 1889 to 1894, a monumental building built by Semper's pupil Otto Wankel until 1890 and then by the head buiding councillor Ottomar Reichelt until 1894. Together with the general ministerial building designed by Waldow and Tscharmann from 1904 to 1906, this building now dominates the view of the Neustadt bank of the Elbe. The gable of the Ministry of Finance bears an indestructible stylised picture under varnish which aims to show the sources of economic and financial resources in Saxony. In the middle is Saxonia, to the right and left are craftsmen, farmers, merchants, miners, scientists, the citizens who create the wealth of the state. Even though opinions on the archetectural and urban design effect have long been divided, the building still has a special feature which was described soon after the turn over the century as a "splendid adornment": a covered skylight. In the GDR period, work was already begun on the restoration of the entrance hall of a side wing true to the original. But only recently has it been possible to undertake a general reconstruction of the building. After the restoration of the interior roof construction, the impressive covered interior courtyard situation was also restored.

Citizen's parks
and citizen awareness

View over the Kreuzkirche (Church of the Cross) to the town hall tower

Every town and city in Germany which can trace its existence back to the Middle Ages has certain features in common. Beside the rights and privileges recorded in official documents and other records these features include outward signs which are immediately visible: the town hall, the wall around the town or city, the market place and the main church at the centre of the town or city. The same applies even today, at least as far as the town hall, the main church and the market place are concerned. The town wall, a sign of the municipal determination to defend its hard-won freedom, disappeared after the end of the 18th or the beginning of the 19th century. Under the changed conditions it was given up, demolished and removed, and the land was then used by the citizens for gardens and parks, and just as frequently for new and generous road systems. But the town hals by the market place and the town chuch dedicated to Our Lady or St. Nicholas remains immovable in its traditional place. In towns and cities which rapidly expanded into the surrounding areas in the second half of the 19th century, where suburbs sprang up like mushrooms and the population increased by several thousand each year, thus causing the municipal population to grow to 100,000 to 200,000 or more, new town halls had to be built to handle the administrative tasks of the municipal community, either directly next to the old town hall, for example in Chemnitz, or, where space did not permit that solution, in a different place, usually at the edge of the old and formerly walled heart of the city, as in Leipzig and Dresden.

But whereas in most towns and cities the town hall was preserved and the new town hall was added, only the new town hall exists in Dresden. In theory, three other town halls should exist – the town hall of Dresden-Neustadt and the two old town halls of Dresden-Altstadt. One of them, which was originally a textile cloth hall and was situated in the middle of the old market, was demolished in 1707 to make room for the ideas of the ruler of the state because the Elector-king needed space for his ring races and carnival events. The town hall built by Johann Christoph Knöffel as a replacement from 1741 to 1745 and paid for by the ruler was destroyed by fire in February 1945, as was the Neustadt town hall which had been rebuilt after the town fire of 1691. The only one remaining is the new town hall designed and built by the architect Karl Roth and the city building councillor Edmund Bräther from 1905 to 1910, a heavy, square-shaped building which is dominated by a thick town hall tower, and which fully met the requirements of municipal administration. When the municipal officials and employees moved into this powerful town hall with its five interior courtyards, the city had already passed the half a million mark in its population growth. There were 551,697 people living in

138,650 residences which were situated in a total of 18,904 residential buildings. In addition there were about 850 public buildings.

The town hall tower, with a height of 98 metres, was a deliberate representation of the citizens in a city which had been "dotted" with state monumental buildings in the decade before and after the turn of the century. The top of the town hall tower is a 4.90 metre high gilded male bronze figure with a wall crown created by the sculptor, Richard Guhr. The building regulations of the city of Dresden had stipulated that no tower was to be higher than the palace tower with its height of 100 metres. As the city wanted to circumnavigate its own regulations, a sculpture was added on top of the tower. The tower with the sculpture is thus 102.90 metres high, and thus the highest tower in the city. The figure, known as the "town hall man" has become a symbol of Dresden. Its counterpart is the companion of Dionysus, Silen, who sits on a donkey in an inebriated condition and invites people to enter the "Rathauskeller" tavern in the basement of the town hall. Its left toe is always polished and shining by the many visitors to the city who want to return some time soon. This sensuous figure was created by Georg Wirba, one of the most important sculptors of the 20th century in Dresden, who was employed as a professor at the Academy of the Arts from 1907 to 1930.

The beautiful view of the Kreuzkirche and the town hall tower will probably no longer be possible after the turn of the millenium because by then, the building work on the southern side of the old market and on Waisenhausstrasse will probably have taken away the generous view that is possible at present.

The Mozart fountain on the Bürgerwiese (citizens' meadow)

Dresden has many fountains and wells which were built on different occasions and for different purposes. Many of them, which simply served to supply water, have ceased to exist since the houses of the city were supplied first with pipe water then, by a sophisticated system of pipes, with drinking water. Today, wells adorn the city in the immediate area around the old market and the palace, in Prager Strasse, in the Neustadt and in park and garden complexes. There is a particularly attractively designed fountain on the way from the new town hall to the large garden along the citizens' meadow. Three golden, shining, graceful female figures dance around a marble column on which the name MOZART is written in simple capital letters. The three figures, which are bathed in water in the warmer seasons of the year, embody cheerfulness, dreaming and gracefulness. Thus, in their own way, they symbolise the musical work of the brilliant composer from Habsburg Austria who, even in his lifetime, had many

followers in the residence city of the Saxon Electors. This city of opera and concerts, where musicians such as Johann Walther, Michael Praetorius, Heinrich Schütz, Johann Adolf Hasse, Carl Maria von Weber, Richard Wagner, Robert Schumann and Richard Strauss were active, did not dedicate any statue or bust to Mozart – instead, it dedicated a fountain. The sculptor Hermann Hosaeus, who lived in Berlin, created it on commission from the Dresden Mozart Association and erected it in the citizens' meadow in 1907.

The fountain is not only a reminder of the works of the Viennese master, which were part of the permanent repertoire of the opera, the state orchestra and the philharmonic orchestra of Dresden, it also commemorates the week which Mozart spent in the city. Together with his friend and sponsor, Duke Karl von Lichnowski, Mozart arrived in Dresden from Prague on 12th April 1789, lodged in the Hotel Pologne in Schloßstrasse and is known to have given two concerts, one in the palace at the invitation of Elector Friedrich August III. That brought him a present from the ruler, "an attractive little box" containing 100 gold ducats. Before Mozart left the city on 18th April on a stagecoach to Leipzig, he accepted invitations to private houses in Dresden and proved his virtuoso ability on the piano. These houses included that of the Russian ambassador and that of the courtly and legal counsellor, Christian Gottfried Körner, a

View over the Kreuzkirche (Church
of the Cross) to the town hall tower

Mozart Fountain on the citizens' meadow

friend of Friedrich Schiller and the father of Theodor Körner. In the house of the Körner family, which was one of the centres of the early Romantic movement in the 1790s and until the Napoleonic period, Mozart was one of the first important guests. Before him, Schiller, Goethe and Kleist had also enjoyed the hospitality of the house.

The Mozart fountain is in a generously designed park complex, the Bürgerwiese (citizens' meadow). From the 15th century, the city had owned an area of land about 1.2 kilometres in length and 90 metres in width along the Kaitzbach stream, which was used as cattle pasture and for making hay and was marked on town maps as the "Inner" and "Outer" citizens' meadow. After the city fortifications were demolished from 1813 onwards and the building area expanded, there was a danger that this meadow area could be built on. To prevent that and preserve the opportunity for the citizens to go for peaceful walks, a passion of the people of Dresden, the city council resolved on 10th February 1838 to convert the citizens' meadow into a park step by step. This began with the "Inner citizens' meadow", which was laid out as a citizens' park up to 1850 according to plans by the court gardener, Terschek. And over 50 years later, the Mozart fountain also found a home in this park. There were lively discussions about the design of the "Outer citizens' meadow" from 1858 onwards, both in the city council and in the "beautification committee" for Dres-

den led by the Foreign and Home Minister, Freiherr Friedrich Ferdinand von Beust. Finally, the famous Prussian general director of gardens, Peter Joseph Lenné, was asked in 1859 to prepare an expert's report. According to his plans, which already included the creation of a zoological garden as an extension of the citizens' meadow, this unique park to serve the people of Dresden was then actually built from 1859 to 1863. Finally, in 1905, the city council resolved that the citizens' meadow should be "permanently excluded from building development". Thus, Dresden today has an artistically designed citizens' park which provides a direct link to the Grosser Garten (large garden).

Grosser Garten (large garden)
Even today, Dresden is not only a city with beautiful Baroque buildings, with theatres and museums, but also a city of beautiful avenues, squares, gardens and parks. Full of buds and blossom in the spring, rich green and full of shade in the summer and beautifully colourful in the autumn – this is the prospect which the city offers to its visitors, both in the old part of the city and at an ever greater distance from the centre. That sets it apart from many other cities and helps to make Dresden one of the most beautiful cities in Europe.

Garden complexes in Dresden were created in the 16th century in front of the fortification embankments of the city. In the

second half of that century, if the early town plans and chronicled records can be trusted, the city was surrounded like a crown by well over 100 "pleasure and kitchen gardens" which belonged to the citizens. After the Thirty Years War, the Elector became involved in this development. It was Johann Georg II, who reigned from 1656 to 1680, who had a suitable setting created outside the palace and the old market for the many courtly festivities and entertainments he organised. As early as 1668, the Elector had purchased a garden in front of the Seetor gate from two Italian singers. Eight years later, on command from the Elector, work began on the design of the Grosser Garten (large garden), which is today actually situated in the city centre if the city, which has greatly expanded since the end of the 19th century, is seen from the air. The farmers of the vilages of Strehlen, Gruna and Striesen had to relinquish fields and meadows. In 1676, Martin Göttler began to design a wooded park on these agricultural areas for the pleasure of the nobility on a square area with sides of about 900 metres. In the middle of this garden, the head state master builder, Johann Georg Starcke, built a palce from 1678 to after 1680 which is regarded as the earliest Baroque building in Electoral Saxony. In 1949, the architectural historian Gerhard Franz wrote: "As a milestone in the development, not only of the Saxon Baroque but of the Baroque in the whole of Germany, it has not yet been recognised and given its due honour." While he was still the Electoral Prince, Johann Georg III took possession of the park, which was initially designed in the Renaissance style. Especially his son, August the Strong, had the park extended from 1698 onwards and converted into a Baroque garden by Johann Friedrich Karcher. In 1719 it was the site of the Venus festival with ladies' ring spearing, theatrical performance and a ball.

The events of war damaged the garden in the course of the 18th and 19th centuries. In December 1745, the park was extensively damaged in connection with the battle of Kesselsdorf, and during the Seven Year War, Prussian troops destroyed the palace, stripped the copper roof, felled several hundred trees and excavated trenches. The park had to be redesigned after this war. That was done by the head state master builder, Julius Heinrich Schwarze, this time in the English style. The Grosser Garten was the battlefield of the battle of Dresden in August 1813, and on 26th August the allies forced the French troops out of the garden. On the afternoon of the same day, the Prussian troops had to yield the terrain they had just gained. After the final victory over Napoleon, the General Governor for Saxony, Duke Repnin, had the severe damage to the garden repaired from 1814 onwards by calling on the services of the farmers, and in part of the Grosser Garten he had an orchard set up.

When the Prussians occupied Dresden in 1866, they felled most of the fruit trees and used them to build a trench. The resulting damage led to the garden being redesigned and significantly extended in the last third of the 19th century. Under the direction of Julius Carl Friedrich Bouché, a pupil of Lenné who was the director of gardens in Dresden from 1873 onwards, the Grosser Garten was brought into the form that it still has today – even though it was devastated by phosphorus and bombs on 14th February 1945 and the buildings in the park, including the palace, were destroyed. The restoration work on the palace which has been in progress since 1954 and frequently interrupted has now at least been completed for the outer facade. As a result, the oldest Baroque building in Dresden which, from 1840 to 1945, housed the museum of the Saxon antiquity association, can again be seen in all its beauty. That also applies to the marble group created around 1720 by Pietro Balestra, "Age abducts beauty", a copy of the original in Farnese Palace in Rome, which was originally erected in the garden of the Japanese Palace and was moved to the Grosser Garten in 1831.

After 1813, further catering establishments were founded in the buildings in the Grosser Garden and the entire garden was made accessible to the general public. The extensive park became a popular excursion destination for young and old, not only at weekends but also on weekday evenings. There were also the popular military concerts. One of the most memorable and momentous military concerts of the 19th century in the Grosser Garten took place on 9th September 1830. A young Saxon official who had just been relocated from Zwickau to Dresden recorded in his diary: "Only a spark was necessary to make this mine explode. Last Thursday, on the 9th of September, I was in the Grosser Garten with the Scholzes and Rosenberger, and there was a concert. Young people requested the Marseilles. It was played over and over again. We went home at about eight, and I had hardly arrived home when a group of people … came down Pirnaische Gasse singing and shouting "Vivat". … I followed them and found the streets full of people." Soon afterwards, the police building and town hall on the old market of Dresden were stormed. It was the beginning of the September uprising of 1830 which led to liberal reforms in Saxony and to the constitutional monarchy with the constitution of 4th September 1831.

The palace in the large garden

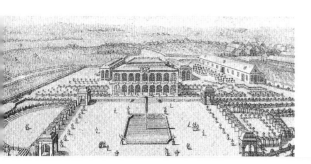

Beyond
the city walls

Herzogin-Garten (Duchess Garden)

On the way from the Zwinger complex to Friedrichstadt along Ostraallee, we now pass a ruined plot of land on which there is only a large portal. It is the last piece of architecture which remains of the Orangerie in the "Herzogin-Garten", and it is largely ignored by local inhabitants and tourists.

Shortly before his death in 1541, Elector Christian I had a garden created outside the Wilsdruff Gate in order to cultivate and care for exotic plants and trees; the garden was known as the "Pomeranzengarten" (Bitter Orange Garden). After the death of the Elector, his wife Sophie von Brandenburg took the garden under her personal administration. The widowed duchess of Saxony now gave the garden her name: the "Herzogin-Garten" (Duchess Garden). The Orangerie building was built by the court master builder Otto von Wolframsdorf, a contemporary and rival of Gottfried Semper. Constructed in the forms of the early Renaissance, it represented an extraordinary addition to the Zwinger and the Semper buildings in the ensemble of royal buildings in the city. In Semper's concept for the design of a Zwinger forum, he had envisaged the construction of a new Orangerie between the court theatre and the Zwinger. As early as 1729 the Orangerie, which was originally accommodated in the arched galleries on the north-west side of Pöppelmann's Zwinger, was moved to the Herzogin-Garten on the command of August the Strong. For continued correct accommodation of the tropical plants which were always particularly popular in Dresden and at court, it was necessary to build a new Orangerie building in the first half of the 19th century. However, because of a decision by the court building authority, this building in the centre of the city was not built in the Zwinger area but a little further away, on the area of a royal garden complex at the beginning of the packing court area and the small Ostra enclosure. For this building, which was built in 1841, the sculptor Ernst Rietschel also created two figures, Pomona and Flora. These were the first works by Rietschel in and for Dresden. The iron foundry of the former cabinet minister, Detlef Graf von Einsiedel in Lauchhammer supplied the artistic cast iron bars.

The Marcolini Palace in Friedrichstadt

At the end of the 17th century, there was still a wide open terrain stretching downstream immediately outside the city fortifications in the broad meander of the Elbe between Dresden and Biesnitz. It was the ducal estate of Ostra which Elector August had established in 1559, and which had become an exemplary estate within just a few years. Grain and cattle pastures, orchards and bee-keeping, diary and hop farming were to be found on this exemplary farm. After 1563, the Elector August gave the estate into the care of his wife, who went into Saxon history as "Mother Anna". The farmers of the village of Ostra had to give up their land to make way for the estate. Eight farming families were settled on the land of the outlying estate of Zschertnitz. Eleven farmers received land from the former monastic estate of Leubnitz, which Duke Moritz had secularised after the Reformation. The farmers moved with all their possessions, even taking the wooden structures of their houses and barns with them, and they founded a new village which they called Neu-Ostra.

After the Thirty Years War, this area outside the city entered a new phase in its development. First of all, Bohemian exiles were settled there. After 1670, Elector Johann Georg II then planned a new suburb for an area of the estate which was close to the city. There was a veritable advertising campaign for the settlement, land plots were provided and a ten year tax exemption was guaranteed. The aim was to attract craft and manufacturing enterprises to settle there and help Dresden to achieve economic growth. In 1678, Johann Daniel Crafft founded the first woollen factory in Saxony, the first nitrate production site was founded in 1692, in 1696 a glassworks was founded, and in 1718 a wax bleaching company. But the settlement concept was still not a complete success. The area became more of a residential area where rich citizens and the court nobility built summer houses and small palaces in order to find peace and relaxation outside the busy residence city. The Marcolini Palace was also built for this purpose. One

of the most influential ministers under August the Strong, Ernst Christoph von Manteuffel, bought a large plot of land in 1718 on which his wife constructed a brewery with the express permission of August the Strong. In 1735 it came into the possession of Count Brühl, who soon sold it back to the Elector at a great profit. Until 1880, the brewery was a popular restaurant in the so-called Friedrichstadt, which had been given this name in 1728 by August the Strong in honour of his son.

A few years after 1718, August the Strong bought the beautiful land plot back from his minister and gave it as a gift to his former mistress, Ursula Katharina von Boccum, Countess Lubomirska, Duchess of Techen, who had married Duke Friedrich Ludwig von Württemberg. She commissioned the head state master builder, Johann Christoph Naumann, to built her a summer palace, and the octagonal hall and the festival hall above it are still part of the Marconlini Palace. The mighty Electoral Saxon Prime Minister, Heinrich von Brühl, bought it from the Württemberg duke and had it extended by the head state master builder Johann Christoph Knöffel, had an Orangerie added and the adjacent large garden area newly designed. The garden, with the Neptune fountain created by Lorenzo Mattielli from 1740 and 1744, which is 40 metres wide and can still be admired as the largest Baroque fountain in Dresden, soon became a well known sight of the residence city of

Dresden. When Brühl died in 1763 and an investigation was instigated against him for malpractice and mismanagement, his Friedrichstadt palace came under compulsory state management, although Brühl's heirs were able to regain it after the investigations were discontinued.

In 1774, Count Camillo Marcolini bought the palace from Brühl's heirs and gave his name to this palace complex. Marcolini was born on 2nd April 1739, and Electoral Prince Friedrich Christian had got to know him during his stay in Rome and appointed him to his court in 1752 as a silver page. There, he became a close friend of the young Friedrich August, the great-grandson of August the Strong, and this friendship resulted in shared political opinions. In 1769 he rose to become the head steward, in 1772 he became a Privy Councillor, in 1778 he became the head chamberlain and in 1780 he became the general director of the art collections and the director of the porcelain manufacturing company, which trusted him with important tasks. Marcolini had his Dresden home converted, fitted out, raised by an extra storey and extended. For more than thirty years, the palace of Count Marcolini became a place for the lively exchange of opinions in the circle of numerous guests and for artistic projects. In 1809 he finally became a cabinet minister and, as such, he initially pursued pro-Napoleonic policies. Nevertheless, fate was not very kind on this wonderful palace and its owner. Just as

Herzogin Garten (Duchess Garden)

The Marcolini Palace

Friedrich the Great had caused the property of his greatest enemy, Heinrich von Brühl, to be attacked, plundered and destroyed in the Seven Years War, so Napoleon was not gentle in his treatment of Marcolini's possessions in 1813. When Napoleon again occupied Saxony in the late spring of 1813, he set up his headquarters in Marcolini's palace. On 28th June 1812, he received the Austrian Foreign Minister, Count Metternich there. After Marcolini died on 10th July 1814 in Prague, the palace remained vacant. In 1835, his son then sold it to the court book printer Werner, who had the palace converted into flats which could be rented out.

In the years before the March revolution of 1848, this palace and the Friedrichstadt became a popular place of residence for artists and university teachers. The sculptor Ernst Julius Hähnel, who worked at the Academy of the Arts from 1854 onwards, set up a studio here, as did the court music director, Richard Wagner. Friedrichstadt was also the area where Johann Andreas Schubert and the writer Ludwig Wittig lived. Wagner composed in his flat in the Marcolini Palace and in his garden house, completing "Lohengrin", drafting the opera "The mines of Falun", which was never finished, and developing the concept for "The Mastersingers" and the "Ring of the Nibelungen". In the months before the May uprising in Dresden, the Marcolini Palace and the surrounding houses became the centre of preparations for the uprising. In March 1849, the Russian revolutionary Michael Bakunin came to Dresden illegally, stayed with Ludwig Wittig in Friedrichstadt and came into close contact with the music director August Röckel. When arguments increased about the acceptance of the Imperial constitution in Saxony on 3rd April 1849 and the Saxon state parliament was finally dissolved on 28th April, one secret meeting was followed by the next. With the final defeat of the armed uprising on 9th May and the escape or arrest of Wagner, Semper, Bakunin, Röckel and Wittig, a deathly calm suddenly came over the Marcolini Palace.

Finally, the city administration purchased the bulding for 62,000 Talers, including the eight hectares of land, and set it up as a municipal hospital, which was urgently needed. The first patients, wounded from the May uprising, were taken into the 53 hospital rooms. The hospital gradually developed to become a medical centre, one extension after the next was added and new specialist clinics arose. Today's municipal hospital in the former Marcolini Palace, together with the Medical Academy in Dresden-Johannstadt, is the largest and most important medical institution in Dresden.

The old Catholic cemetery in Friedrichstadt

Directly opposite the Marcolini Palace, a large portal leads into a cemetery which is separated from the road by a high wall. It is the old Catholic cemetery, and like the Schlosskirche (Palace Church) it is a special element in the residence city of Protestant Saxony. In 1720 the Saxon Elector Friedrich August I, who had converted to Catholicism in 1697, had to issue a degree to enable deceased adherents of the Catholic faith to be buried in Dresden. It was not possible to carry out this decree inside the city, but it was possible in the developing suburb on part of the Ostra estate. Even then, the statute was linked with strict regulations for the constantly growing Catholic community. The construction of a chapel was forbidden "for eternal times". This prohibition was only revoked in 1842 after the constitution had assured freedom of conscience. It was expressly forbidden to celebrate funerals "with pomp".

From 1721, there was again a Catholic cemetery in the Electorate of Saxony for the first time since the introduction of the Reformation in 1539. Today it is the second oldest cemetery in the city after the Elias Cemetery at Sachsenplatz, and it is a special place where the fleeting nature of human life, in its own way, represents an aspect of cultural history. This is especially true because of the fact that the Saxon Elector and Polish King brought artists, sculptors, painters, composers and singers to Dresden from Italy, Bavaria, Austria and France to adorn his residence and that some of them ended their lives in the city and found their last place of rest on the only Catholic cemetery in the city. This was true of

Balthasar Permoser, Johann Baptist Casanova and a number of Polish magnates and their wives. A son of the Elector from his liaison with Ursula Katharina Lubomirska, the Saxon general Johann Georg Chevalier de Saxe, is also buried there. The writer Friedrich Schlegel, the Romantic painter Gerhard von Kügelgen and the tenor Josef Tichatschek were laid to rest there.

There is a special story surrounding the grave of the musician Carl Maria von Weber on the north side of the cemetery. Weber was in Dresden in 1811 and gave a piano concert – without success. He then said that this city would never see him again, but five years later he accepted a call to Dresden and became the director of the German Opera House. After his induction on 17th January 1817, Dresden became a centre for German Romantic opera in spite of all its opponents and in competition with the predominant Italian opera. During his years in Dresden, Weber composed "Der Freischütz" (The Freeshooter), "Euryanthe" and "Oberon". On a long visit to England where he had an attractive financial offer from the Covent Garden Opera, Weber died in London on 5th June 1826. His widow in Dresden did not have enough money to have his body brought back to Dresden, so he was buried in the crypt of Moorsfield Chapel. On 16th Febuary 1841, an article was published in Dresden about the alleged impending clearing out of the crypt. That

gave an impetus for the mortal remains of Weber to be brought back to Dresden. A committee was formed for the purpose at the beginning of March 1841, and on 26th March the first concert of the "Dresdner Liedertafel" (Dresden Song Table) was given to raise the funds necessary to return the body. When Richard Wagner was appointed as the court director of music in 1842, he took up the idea of returning the body and became its fiercest advocate. After many efforts, Wagner and his friend Ferdinand Heine obtained royal permission on 22nd March 1844. The coffin arrived in Dresden by boat in December 1844. Weber's oldest son, the engineer Max Weber who was so successful later on, had arranged the formalities in London and accompanied the transport. In a solemn funeral which was followed with great interest on the part of the Dresden public, Weber was buried in the old Catholic cemetery on 16th December 1844. Gottfried Semper, a friend of Wagner's, had created the simple memorial stone. Richard Wagner, who had composed the funeral music from two motifs out of Weber's "Euryanthe", wrote about this unusual event in his memoirs: "After we had taken our leave of the coffin in the small memorial chapel of the Catholic cemetery in Friedrichstadt, where it was quietly and humbly received with a wreath by Frau Devrient, the coffin was then ceremoniously lowered on the following day into the grave provided by us".

Dresden Harbour

Shipping and trade on the Elbe have always been important for the city and the state. The natural waterway from Bohemia to the North Sea was a vital transport route, although the trading places along the Elbe continually dwindled. For many centuries, for example, Pirna with its trading rights was much more important than Dresden. It was only when the Saxon Elector succeeded in shifting this privilege to Dresden that the residence city also gained in importance as a shipping port and a cargo loading site.

In view of the industrialisation of Saxony in the 19th century, the resulting rapid increase in the turnover of goods through Hamburg to all continents and the constant increase in the number of steamships since the middle of this century, plans were soon made to build a new harbour. In view of the natural terrain, the area of the large Ostra enclosure was a logical choice. This was supported by the discussions on the possibility of moving the Weisseritz stream further down the Elbe at the edge of the old part of the city, an idea which had been under consideration since the great flood of March 1845. In connection with the extension of the railway network in Dresden, the surveyor Moritz Pressler suggested that a new main station and a new harbour should be created by moving the Weisseritz stream westwards to enter the Elbe at a point which remained to be constructed, and he prepared plans

The old Catholic cemetery
in Friedrichstadt

A grave in the old Catholic cemetery

accordingly. When the reorganisation of the railway system in Dresden was urgently necessary towards the end of the 19th century, Pressler's plans were taken up, and work began in 1873.

In 1891 numerous building workers, supported by steam-powered excavating machines, began to dig out a new river bed for the Weisseritz between Löbtau and Cotta. The mouth of the Weisseritz, the most important tributary of the Elbe in the city, was moved three kilometres downstream along the Elbe. In the same process, a new harbour was built near the mouth of the Weisseritz. Two dry excavators worked there and excavated a total of 1.5 million cubic metres of earth. Between 1891 and 1895, a harbour area was created which was 150 metres wide and about 1100 metres long, with a bed that is two metres below the lowest water level of the Elbe registered in 1904, but with its quay walls 30 centimetres above the highest water level that had ever been measured on the Elbe in Dresden, i.e. the water level of the flood of 31st March 1845. With the relocation of the Weisseritz and the construction of the harbour, a third major construction project was also carried out: the creation of the flood channel through the large Ostra enclosure. The new harbour itself was taken into operation on 1st November 1891 as the "King Albert Harbour". Up to 25 cargo ships could dock at the same time. In the first year of operation, 150,000 tonnes of goods were handled.

Three years later, the turnover of goods had already reached 320,000 tonnes. At the same time, convenient railway links were laid. A number of new transport and industrial companies settled in the harbour area. A new tank depot was built. From 1912 to 1914, the Bienert brothers had a new mill, the harbour mill constructed by the Lossow and Kühne architectural office. The silo building and the 64 metre high silo tower could hold 130,000 tonnes of grain. This made the Elbe harbour in Dresden the largest German site for handling overseas grain before the First World War.

All of these facilities still exist today and characterise this part of the city as an important element in the economic life of the city. Today, the harbour is suffering from the shift of freight transport to the roads. In spite of all the efforts of the monument conservation authorities, this will cause the Dresden Elbe harbour basin to be reduced in size during the coming years, which means that the original structure with the end of the harbour will be loss. As a result, Dresden will lose an important industrial monument.

View of the Elbe at Pieschener Winkel (Pieschen Corner)

There are only three points in the city of Dresden from which the beholder of our days can enjoy an impressive view of the large meanders of the Elbe. In addition to the well-known view from the Wald-

schlösschen (woodland castle), the other main view is at the so-called Pieschener Winkel (Pieschen corner). It is downstream on the Elbe opposite the large Ostra enclosure, and its name is derived from the community of Pieschen, a local community which was first mentioned in documents in 1292. It was a farming village with an extensive field system and vineyards in front of the gates of the residence city. In the first official population census in 1834, the village had 347 inhabitants and about 80 farms. With the rapid industrial development in the second half of the 19th century, Pieschen was one of the first suburbs of Dresden to develop into a residential area for the workers. The fields successively disappeared and were replaced by three-storey residential buildings. Soon, built-up roads were the dominant feature in the area. The population grew accordingly, and in 1867 there were 1425 inhabitants. In 1880 the population had grown to 6,000, ten years later the figure had more than doubled to 12,400, and on the eve of the First World War more than 33,000 people lived in the suburb, which had been part of Dresden since 1897. In 1893, the communal administration itself had applied to be incorporated into the city to avoid serious financial difficulties because the number of low income workers living in the area meant that the tax revenue was below average.

The development of the area in the 19th century had been influenced by its favourable transport location. The construction

Dresden Harbour

View of the Elbe at Pieschener Winkel
(Pieschen Corner)

route for the first long-distance railway in Germany from Dresden to Leipzig went through Pieschen. The surveyors who arrived in 1835 were threatened with violence by Pieschen's farmers, but they were not able to prevent the construction of the railway. The Elbe harbour was built on Pieschen land from 1856 to 1859, and it is still used as a winter storage area for paddle steamers of the "Weisse Flotte" (White fleet). From 1881, the area was linked with the city by one of Dresden's first horse-drawn carriage routes, which formed the basis for the electric tram line from Dresden Postplatz via Pieschen to Mickten, which was commissioned in 1899. These transport links also included the establishment of a ferry across the Elbe from Pieschener Winkel (Pieschen corner) to the slaughterhouse building in the Ostra enclosure and the industrial companies situated there. For the people who lived in Pieschen and worked in the industrial area of Friedrichstadt and Löbtau, the ferry was their only connection to their place of work. The idyllic view of the Elbe ferry, the Elbe river and the slaughterhouse island does not betray this original purpose.

Übigau

On the right bank of the Elbe, directly opposite the Friedrichstadt bank on the Kaditz "elbow", Übigau is situated on a small flat area that is not subject to floods. The village, which was first mentioned in documents at the beginning of the 14th century, had six farms. Situated on the so-called bishop's route – the road link of the Meissen bishops from Meissen to their lands in and around Stolpen – it led a calm and peaceful existence even into the 18th century. Then lively building activities began. Count Jakob Heinrich von Flemming, who was a Pommeranian by birth and soon became the most influential and important minister of August the Strong after he had successfully promoted August's election as the Polish king in 1697, had his new summer residence built relatively far downstream in largely unspoiled Elbe scenery – Übigau Palace. For this pleasure palace and the small French-style park, four vineyard farmers had to sell their property. It was built from 1724 to 1726 by Johann Friedrich von Eosander, known as Göthe, for Flemming, who had to have a second palace of this type built for himself near Dresden. Flemming, a regional minister in the Privy Cabinet and a General Field Marshall, was hardly able to use the Übigau pleasure palace because he died two years after its completion. This estate was also purchased by the Elector. Under his son, Elector Friedrich August II, it became the scene of just a few court festivities and of a military exercise camp held in 1753.

After the Seven Years War, when even the Electoral court was forced to make economies, the estate remained unused. It was neglected and became derelict. The Dresden Council master carpenter, Paul Sieber, purchased the pleasure palace, and later it was used by the "Dresdner Actien-Maschinenbau-Verein" (Dresden shareholding engineering association), which was founded in 1836 by Johann Andreas Schubert and Wilhelm August Lohrmann, as their administrative building. On this estate, Schubert built the first German steam locomotive, the "Saxonia", and the first paddle steamers for shipping on the Elbe. From 1877 it became the location of a shipbuilding yard – of which one crane has been preserved as a symbolic technical monument.

Friedrichstadt shunting and switching yard

The age of machinery and technical progress was not only heralded by the increasing number of factories with their smoky chimney stacks – the ribbons of steel which increasingly crossed through the land also became a symbol of development. On 18th July 1833, Friedrich List presented the public in Leipzig with a tract entitled: "On a Saxon iron railway system as a basis for a general German railway, and especially on the design of a railway from Leipzig to Dresden". In the same year, a committee was formed in Leipzig under the name: "Committee to prepare the construction of the railway", and its application to build the first German long distance rail connection between Dresden and Leipzig was approved in May 1834 by the Saxon government. After the surveying work had been completed, railway construction started from Leipzig and from Dresden. Shortly after nine o'clock

A crane near Übigau

Schloss Übigau (Übigau Palace)

on the morning of 8th April 1839, the festively decorated passenger train bearing King Friedrich August II set out from the Leipzig station in Dresden-Neustadt, and it arrived in Leipzig a few hours later. On the intervention of Prince Johann, the first German steam locomotive built by Schubert in Übigau and bearing the name "Saxonia" was permitted to follow it. On the return journey, the first act of sabotage in German railway history was committed. In Priestewitz, Schubert's locomotive was prevented from continuing the journey by a wrong points setting.

The successful operation of the railway led to the construction of new rail links in Saxony soon after, particularly because the surveying work had already been done. In the summer of 1844, excavation work began on the construction of the Saxon-Silesian railway, and soon afterwards the routes from Dresden to Chemnitz and Zwickau, from Zwickau to Leipzig, the Chemnitz-Riesa railway and the Saxon-Bohemian railway were taken into operation. After the middle of the century, Dresden was the most important railway junction in Europe. With a second bridge construction project in Dresden, which was also used for the railway, the connection was made across the Elbe. The Marienbrücke bridge built between 1846 and 1852 linked the Dresden-Leipzig and Saxon-Silesian railway with the Saxon-Bohemian railway. In the last third of the 19th century, the railway facilities in the city

were further modernised, which meant a complete reorganisation of the railway system. From 1892, railway tracks were laid from Strehlen to the Hauptbahnhof (main station), and the main Dresden station was built on the model of the Gare du Nord in Paris. The same also happened in Dresden-Neustadt.

In addition, a large shunting yard was built in order to be able to handle the enormously increased volume of rail traffic. In connection with the relocation of the Weisseritz stream and the Elbe harbour, the intricate rail network of the Friedrichstadt railway complex was created. The approximately 1.5 million cubic metres of excavated earth from the construction of the harbouir and the flood channel were used to redesign the area of the Friedrichstadt goods station. The incline with a length of 2.5 kilometres and a height of up to 17 metres above street level was created. Goods trains arrive, are recombined by destination, then leave the shunting yard to the north, south, east and west. From here, "container trains" set out through the valley of the Elbe to Lobositz and arrive from there. The technological transport system developed by Dresden's engineers over a hundred years ago is still effective today.

View of the "Yenidze"
Since the autumn of 1996, when the scaffolding came down from a building that is on the border between the city centre and

Friedrichstadt and is directly next to the railway line from Dresden-Hauptbahnhof to Dresden-Neustadt, this building has attracted attention even from a distance. The large dome made entirely of yellow glass and the minaret-style chimney stretching up into the sky do not seem to belong in this urban landscape, and they provoke the often-heard question: "What is it?" If we ask the children of Dresden, we will perhaps be told that it is the "cigarette church". There is a grain of truth in this term because the building is used for cigarette production and the architectural style is based on that of a mosque.

In 1862, a French businessman moved his cigarette production operations from St. Petersburg to Dresden and opened the first cigarette factory in Germany under the name "Compagnie Laferme". Soon, this branch of the consumer goods industry became at home in Dresden, and alongside the rapidly developing fine mechanics and optical industry, the chemical and pharmaceutical industry and the production of sewing machines, it became an important sector of Dresden's manufacturing industry. Further cigarette factories were built after 1862, and one of them in 1866 was the "Oriental Tobacco and Cigarette Factory Yenidze" belonging to the cigarette manufacturer Hugo Zietz. The name came from a small local community in one of the most important tobacco-growing areas in Turkey. Within just a few years, with a profit

Friedrichstadt shunting and
switching yard

View of the "Yenidze"

margin of about ninety per cent, Zeitz earned a fortune which enabled him to build a new factory after the turn of the century. The commission was given to the young architect, Martin Hammitzsch, who joined the "NS" movement in the Weimar Republic, made himself a career after 1933 and rose to become the director of the Dresden State Building Academy. Finally he became a brother-in-law of Adolf Hitler when he married his half-sister, Angela Rambal.

The "Yenidze" stands on the old river bed of the Weisseritz which was filled in after 1893. The Oriental and Byzantine external appearance was only the facade for what was, at the time, the most modern of factories, and at the same time, a high social standard was aimed for in the construction. It was one of the first steel frame buildings in Germany, and on the fifth floor it had a kitchen and dining room for a thousand workers. In addition, there was a bath complex which the workers could use free of charge. The dome area contained a respite area for men and women where periodicals, deck chairs and folding beds were available for the relaxation of the employees during their breaks. A Dresden architectural historian commented on this building a few years ago: "All of the things demanded by Gropius for the design of the workplace in 1911 were fulfilled here by Zietz and Hammitzsch in 1907."

Across the Augustusbrücke (Augustus Bridge)

The Golden Rider

If we walk from Schlossplatz across the Augustus Bridge towards the Neustadt area, we are crossing the oldest bridge in the city. Built in stone shortly after the year 1200, after its third extension in 1343 it had 24 pillars and 23 arches. 200 years later, when Duke Moritz had the fortifications of the city moved to the Elbe, five pillars and four arches were filled in. The bridge remained in this form until the first third of the 18th century. Then the bridge was no longer adequate for its purpose, particularly as inspections revealed that twelve of the pillars had lost their stability. As the city had no money for repairs – not to mention the construction of a new bridge – August the Strong undertook the construction work, which cost him about 57,000 Talers. In 1728 his head state master builder, Pöppelmann, received the commission to carry out building work on the bridge. The rebuilding was carried out in only sixteen months, the bridge was made higher and wider so that it was possible for two carriages to pass and, in addition, for footpaths to be laid out to the right and left. Alongside the bridge over the Vitava (Moldau) in Prague and the bridge over the Danube in Regensburg, the Augustus Bridge was now acknowledged as one of the most beautiful and powerful bridge buildings in Europe. Hans Christian Andersen expressed his impression on his journey to the Sächsische Schweiz (Little Switzerland in Saxony) in the summer of

1831 in the following words: "When I came to the Augustus Bridge, which I already knew well from copper engravings and paintings, it seemed as if I had been here earlier in a dream". The bridge had to be demolished in 1907 to make way for a new bridge, but the new bridge integrated the forms created by Pöppelmann.

In 1730 it was planned to decorate the bridge with a riding statue of August the Strong. This was under discussion from 1704 onwards, and Paul Heermann modelled a riding statue in 1722. A wooden model of this statue was placed on the fifth pillar of the bridge on 19th April 1730 for inspection by the Elector/king. In the same year, Zacharias Longuelune proposed a plan to place the riding statue on the Blockhaus. Both suggestions were rejected. Three years after the death of August the Strong, the riding statue was given its permanent site in front of the Blockhaus on Neustadt market. Longuelune designed the pedestal, the colonel and coppersmith Ludwig Winckelmann cast the statue in copper, and it was then plated with gold.

August the Strong, who was the Elector of Saxony from 1694 and the king of Poland from 1697 until his death on 1st February 1733 in Warsaw, rides away from the Augustus Bridge into the new royal city, which had borne the name of Neustadt (new city) since 1732, and his gaze is directed to the east towards his kingdom. Perhaps the posture and expression of the statue with

Golden rider

Japanese Palace
(now Saxon Early History Museum and
Museum of Ethnology)

View of the Dreikönigskirche
(Church of the Three Kings) from Königstrasse

the curvetting horse also express more: the dream of the Imperial throne, which had not yet been relinquished. The monument, a symbol of Baroque and royal Dresden, was safeguarded from destruction in 1944 and reinstalled in 1956 after the gold plating had been restored.

Japanese Palace

The bank of the Elbe on the Neustadt side between the Augustus Bridge and Marienbrücke is a prominent part of Dresden-Neustadt – actually, it is the area of Altendresden on the right bank, which was first mentioned in written records in 1350. Its origin was the Slavic settlement of Drezdáne. The community was granted municipal rights in 1403, and in 1404 it became the site of an Augustine monastery which was founded by Margrave Wilhelm I and demolished after the introduction of the Reformation in 1546. Under Duke/Elector Moritz, the town area on the right bank of the Elbe – which was merged with the town of Neuendresden on the left bank of the Elbe in 1549 – was surrounded with its first fortifications, which were strengthened in the Thirty Years War and before 1684 by Wolf Caspar von Klengel. A devastating fire which broke out in the house of the cabinetmaker Tobias Edler in Meissnische Gasse on 6th August 1685 almost completely destroyed the city. For the reconstruction, Klengel designed a generous plan on the principle of a Baroque town. Breite Strasse,

beginning from the Augustus Bridge, was to characterise the city. When August the Strong began his reign in 1694, only a third of the city had been rebuilt. The continuation of the building work was simplified in 1714 and 1720 by building regulations. Königstrasse, Hauptstrasse, Obergraben and Niedergraben were largely built in the form that is still preserved today. Since the 18th century, four large buildings have dominated the visual appearance of the area: the Blockhaus at the Neustadt end of the Augustus Bridge, the Neustadt town hall built from 1750 to 1754, the Dreikönigskirche (Church of the Three Kings) and the Japanese Palace.

The powerful minister of the Elector/king, Jakob Heinrich Graf von Flemming, had purchased a large area of land by the Elbe and had a land house built there in 1715, which he soon let out to the Dutch ambassador. The palace thus acquired its first name, the Holland Palace. In 1717, August the Strong bought the residence from his minister. Matthäus Daniel Pöppelmann, Jean de Bodt and Zacharias Longuelune had to convert it for August the Strong and create a palace building with four wings in which he wanted to accommodate his porcelain collection. East Indian, Chinese and Japanese porcelain was highly regarded among the European court nobility. In return for such porcelain, whole regiments were hired or even sold to foreign powers. The Albertine Wettin dynasty were

no exception. An added element was the fact that the porcelain factory founded in 1710 in the Albrechtsburg in Meissen was the first factory in Europe which was able to fire hard porcelain, under the direction of Johann Friedrich Böttger, which was not inferior to "East Indian" porcelain in any way. But although there were plans for an appropriate interior design of the palace, they were never carried out. After it had been used for a variety of purposes, the building, which had changed its name to "Japanese Palace", was rebuilt for the purposes of the royal library, which had been founded by Elector August around 1560. An inscription was added to the gable which can today again be seen in golden letters: MUSEUM USUI PUBLICO PATENS – museum open for public use. The building is no longer a library, but it still serves as a museum – after 1945, the State Prehistoric and Early History Museum and the Museum of Ethnology found a home there. The French park designed between the building and the Elbe in the 18th century is no longer there, in its place there is an English-style park.

View of the Dreikönigskirche (Church of the Three Kings) from Königstrasse

After the great fire of 1685, which also destroyed the church of Altendresden, the church, which had first been given the name of Dreikönigskirche in 1421, was rebuilt on its old site three years later, in 1688. It was situated in the middle of what is now Haupt-

The Thomae altar
in the
Dreikönigskirche
(Church of
the Three Kings)

strasse. When Klengel's plans for the construction of the "new king's city" were implemented after 1714, envisaging a road at the Neustadt market which was 500 metres long and 57 metres wide, narrowing to 38 metres at the Black Gate, the church was in the way. As years of negotiations by the Electoral Saxon building office and the Privy Council with the city and the church community did not lead to an agreement on the relocation of the church, August the Strong issued an order two years before his death for the church to be demolished and rebuilt at the expense of the state on a different site. From 1731 to 1739, the Dreikönigskirche was built to plans by Pöppelmann and Bähr by the council master bricklayer Gottfried Fehre. As the main entrance was to be from Hauptstrasse, this meant that the altar had to be moved to the western end of the nave, which was a departure from European tradition. The sandstone altar, which survived the bomb raids in 1945 without any damage and could thus be erected again, is 16 metres high. The altar was created by the sculptor Johann Benjamin Thomae, who lived in Hauptstrasse and was one of the best pupils of Balthasar Permoser. The icons depict the parable of the wise and foolish virgins combined with the appearance of the star of Bethlehem. This imagery, which is partly in the form of free-standing sculptures, is framed by the evangelists Matthew and John.

The Dreikönigskirche, the spire of which had only been built from 1854 to 1857, was destroyed in 1945, and only the outer walls were left standing. The building permission for reconstruction was only granted by the council of the city of Dresden in 1977, and the foundation stone was laid in 1984. The aim was to permit dual use as a church social centre and a local church building. The church social centre was opened with a large assembly hall on 9th September 1990. This was just at the right time because the Saxon federal state parliament, which was to be elected on 17th October 1990, urgently needed a suitable room to meet in. They use the festival room, which is adorned by a large mural by Werner Juza on the subject of "Reconciliation". In their first period of office – during which hard work was necessary to lay the legal groundwork for the Free State of Saxony – the members of the state parliament met under this mural until they could move into the state parliament building in 1993.

The fountain "Stürmische Wogen" (Stormy waves) on Albertplatz

On commission from the city council the sculptor Robert Diez, who was a professor at the Academy of the Arts from 1891, designed two elaborate fountains for Bautzner Platz, now Albertplatz – "Stilles Wasser" (Still water) on the east of the square and "Stürmische Wogen" (Stormy waves) on the west of the square. In 1909, the art historian

Paul Schumann gave the following rather poetic description of these outstanding works of art: "An imaginative design shows on the one side the peaceful sea, on the other side the wild sea – the vivid figures capture the moods of the sensitive beholder of the sea. Majestic vastness, glistening beauty, cheerful delight and whimsical meditation are embodied in the fish-tailed mermaid with the lyre, in the groups made up of pearl and nymph, mermaid and nix, water lily and sleeping boy. And on the other hand we see the storm rushing on a powerful charging horse over the mighty foaming waves, then the warrior using a sharp shell to assail the enormous catfish, the roaring of the breakers, the fight of the two mermen for the sea star and the handsome youth carried up from the depths by the waves."

The two fountains were erected in the middle of a newly designed park complex in 1893 after ten years of work. Whereas the "Stilles Wasser" (Still water) remained in place after 1945, the "Stürmische Wogen" (Stormy waves), which had been damaged by bombing in February 1945, was replaced by a different monument. From 7th November 1945 until 1992, its place was taken by the "Soviet Memorial" by the Dresden sculptor Otto Rost, which commemorated the march of Red Army troops into Dresden on 8th May 1945. From the unveiling of the memorial until 1989, there were two or sometimes three state-ordained wreath-laying ceremonies each year at this statue – on 21st

The fountain "Stürmische Wogen"
(Stormy Waves) on Albertplatz

February (?), 8th May and 7th November. Since 1993, the "Stürmische Wogen" have been in their old place again, which restored Albertplatz to some of its original beauty.

For centuries, Dresden-Neustadt was surrounded by a tight ring of monumental fortifications, town walls, ramparts and town gates. This changed when Napoleon commanded in 1809 that the fortifications of Dresden should be pulled down. This demolition work, which lasted from 1817 to 1831, was directed by the court master builder Thormeyer. The land covered by the fortifications was generously redesigned. In front of the Black Gate, Bautzner Platz was built, and new streets radiated from it. As a result, Dresden for the first time had a systematically implemented open building structure forming a wide green belt around Neustadt, from Leipziger Strasse where it enters the city, with the two gatehouses by Thormeyer, via Bautzner Platz to the Elbe.

For the development of Dresden's visual appearance, the removal of the fortification walls brought another typical element. Not only did the city open up to the surrounding landscape – the landscape itself entered the city. Because there was now sufficient building land, detached residential houses became dominant in the urban structure. There arose streets with detached buildings surrounded by gardens and bordered by fences. This can still be seen especially in the area around Albertplatz.

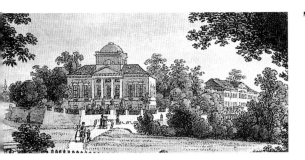

The "other city"

The old Jewish cemetery

The mediaeval city of Dresden had its own Jewish community. The name of Jüdenhof (Jewish court) is preserved in the architecture of the city. There are stories of persecution of the Jews in times of plague because the Jews were blamed for such catastrophes. In the plague year of 1349, all the Jews of Dresden were apparently burned on the old market place with the approval of the Wettin Margrave Friedrich II. At the end of the 17th century, there were still no people of the Jewish faith living in Dresden. It was only during the reign of August the Strong that individual Jews came to the Electoral Saxon court with their families. Their residence in the city was regulated by an Electoral Saxon decree of 1746. Strict limitations were placed on their employment and economic activities, their religious life and their position in society, but their existence in the city was marked by tolerance on the part of the responsible bodies in society. This included the allocation of two land plots in the outer part of Neustadt at the edge of Dresden Heath by the Priessnitz stream, relatively far from the city walls, for the burial of deceased Jewish citizens. Thus, a Jewish cemetery was established which was used by the Jewish community in Dresden until 1868. At the end of the Seven Years War there were 809 Jews living in Dresden, in 1832 there were 874. On the basis of the religious freedom guaranteed in the constitution of 4th September 1831, the "Act relating to the civil status of the Jews" of 18th May 1837 and the "Act concerning a number of modifications in the civil status of the Jews" of 16th August 1838 granted fully equal rights to the Jews in Saxony. It was only on the basis of these acts that the Jewish community in Dresden was able to build its own synagogue. Gottfried Semper was the architect and master builder for the Dresden synagogue, which was consecrated on 8th May 1840 with the participation of prominent representatives of the state, the city and the Protestant and Catholic church, and which was consumed by flames in the "Kristallnacht" (Crystal night) on 9th November 1938. The star of David on Semper's synagogue was secretly rescued by a Dresden fireman, and after 1945 it was returned to the Jewish community and mounted on the hall of the new Jewish cemetery in Johannstadt, which was established in 1866 and is still used as a synagogue.

Looking into Louisenstrasse

If we go north from Albertplatz, we come to "Outer Neustadt". Between Königsbrücker Strasse and the Priessnitz stream, Bautzner Strasse and Alaunplatz there are streets with crumbling facades, doors and windows sealed off with red bricks, and in between there are individual buildings which have already been renovated – in their restored beauty they do not seem to fit into this part of the city. In the evening and at night, this area around Louisenstrasse, Böhmische

The old Jewish cemetery

Looking into Louisenstrasse

Strasse, Martin-Luther-Platz, Rothenburger Strasse and Görlitzer Strasse comes to life. The taverns, cafés, pubs and pizza restaurants are full of voices and pop music, a scene that is largely dominated by young people. Some people speak of the "Scene", of the people who live or meet in the "colourful town". Among them are perhaps painters, poets and musicians who will become masters of their art – like Erich Kästner, who was born in Königsbrücker Strasse and who describes this area in which he grew up in his memoirs "When I was a small boy".

In the 18th century, this area was still open countryside stretching to Dresden Heath, which extended to what is now Alaunplatz and was called "Auf dem Sande" (On the sand). When many of the people of Dresden lost their houses in 1760 through the Prussian bombardment, they settled in this area. They included Protestant refugees from Bohemia who called their street "Böhmische Strasse". There were also a few isolated businesses such as an alumn boilery on the border between the "sand" and Dresden Heath. The names of Alaunstrasse and Alaunplatz (Alumn Street/Square) are the only reminders of this boilery. When the head state master builder Johann Gottlob Hartmann planned and constructed the generously designed Bautzner Platz outside the Black Gate from 1817 to 1831, this new area became directly involved in the rapid expansion of the city caused by the fast

growth in the population. In 1830 there were already 354 residential buildings and about 3700 inhabitants. In 1835, the new area was given the name of Antonstadt and incorporated into Dresden. On the Neustadt side it was the first area incorporated into the city after the removal of the city walls.

In the second half of the 19th century, this sparsely populated area was made into a residential area for the workers, and shortly before the First World War 56,000 people lived here. The narrow, treeless roads with two, three and four-storey residential buildings in an unbroken line along the street front and with rear buildings and rear courtyards can still be seen today, but most of the people have moved away during the last 20 years. In "Outer Neustadt", the Baroque city of Dresden, which is often seen only from its more attractive sides, also has a less attractive district like any other large city in Europe.

Pfunds Molkerei (Pfund's Dairy)

On the way out of the city on the Neustadt side, shortly before Bautzner Strasse crosses the Priessnitz, the most beautiful milk shop in the world can be found on the right of the street. When we enter this shop, we are in a large, completely tiled room. Not only the walls and floor are lined with colourful tiles – the ceiling, counter, till and refrigerator are also tiled. In the elegant main building of the "Dresden Dairy of the Pfund

Brothers", which was built in 1891 at Bautzner Strasse 79, a milk shop was created which was designed by the world-famous Dresden tile, ceramics and porcelain firm of Villeroy & Boch with hand-painted tiles by Dresden artists. Everything connected with milk production and refinement can be seen, surrounded by draped blossoms, ornaments and presented by nymphs who symbolise children and healthy child nutrition. Almost forgotten and close to dereliction at the end of the GDR period, an extensive restoration with a great deal of skilful craftsmanship and artistry and an enormous amount of work and expense enabled the shop to be opened again on 16th October 1995 for the sale and consumption of milk products, especially French cheese specialities. Almost everything is now in its original condition, but the Pfund milk products are unfortunately no longer available because production ended in the 1970s and the production site was demolished from 1978 onwards.

The "milk Empire" of the Pfund brothers, which was famous after 1900 and had its headquarters in Dresden, started in a very simple way. The Saxon state capital, which was bursting at the seams in the last third of the 19th century in view of the population explosion, had to be supplied with everything, especially food. People came into Dresden from all over the surrounding area with carrier baskets, hand carts, wheelbarrows, dog-drawn carts and horse-drawn

Pfunds Molkerei (Pfund's Dairy)

carriages to supply the city with food. The milk which was so important, especially for children and those who were ill, came once a day in open carriages and was poorly cooled or not cooled at all. The carriages then left the city loaded with rubbish. The whole procedure was not exactly an example of hygiene. In 1879 Paul Pfund, who owned a farm in Reinholdshain near Dippoldiswalde, set out for Dresden with his wife, six cows and six pigs. In "Outer Neustadt", which was developing to a workers' residential area, he found accommodation in Görlitzer Strasse, opened a milk shop there and sold milk fresh from the cow. The customers could watch the cows being milked through a window in the shop.

Business was flourishing, and before long it was necessary for the business to expand considerably. Pfund purchased extra land in Bautzner Strasse and built up the company into a modern dairy factory of world-wide renown. In 1880 he sold 150 litres of milk per day, by the end of the Weimar Republic, Pfund's Dairy processed up to 60,000 litres per day. Paul Pfund, who died in 1923 in Dresden, was not only a milk producer. He was also an inventor and a pioneer of modern milk processing. He was the first to produce condensed milk in Germany, and he sold it throughout the world. He developed child foods with a quality comparable to mother's milk, a milk-based soap for sensitive skin, and in 1900 he introduced pasteurisation for all milk products. He was

awarded the title of a distinguished royal Saxon merchant, and he soon added a number of workshops to his dairy in order to become independent of outside suppliers – a cardboard factory, a label printing shop, a metalworking shop, a tinning shop for milk containers, a smithy for 100 horses and the milk carriages, a painting shop for the milk carriages, a carpentry shop, a cabinet-making shop, a carriage building shop and even his own tailor's shop for the uniforms of his coachmen. The size and production volume of the company reduced slowly during the Second World War. The nationalisation of Pfund's Dairy in 1972 led to the end of milk processing in this traditional firm after it had existed for a hundred years. What remains is the memory and the most beautiful milk shop in the world.

Up the Elbe to Loschwitz

Schloss Albrechtsberg (Albrechtsberg Palace)

This is a place which is designed "to enjoy the view and walk in the bright cloisters half way between heaven and earth". Built in three steps leading up from the Elbe, at a height of 45 metres up the river bank, Albrecht Palace is still standing today. This palace and two other palace-type buildings in the immediate vicinity, Villa Stockhausen and Eckberg Palace, are presented to the daily tourists as the "Albrecht palaces". They are beautiful and majestic to behold, protruding from the greenery of the Elbe bank slope. All three buildings were built between 1850 and 1860, Albrechtsberg Palace and Villa Stockhausen "in the Hellenist style of Schinkel", Eckberg Palace in the English Tudor style.

In the 19th century there were still vineyards on the slopes of the Elbe, and they only failed after the vine pest attack in 1886. Apart from the slope below Villa Stockhausen, which was again established as a vineyard by the cultural association in the middle of the 1980s, the slopes have been wooded with deciduous trees since then. The vineyards on this part of the Elbe just above Dresden must have been idyllic in appearance. The Scottish peer, Lord Jacob of Findlater, was so enthusiastic that he bought a large part of the slope of the Elbe and had a "vineyard palace" built among the vines by Johann August Griesel, a pupil of Krubsacius. When the palace was complete in 1811, its owner died without ever moving in. Ten years later, his heirs established a guest house in the "most beautiful residential palace in Dresden", and in the 1820s, 1830s and 1840s it was the most popular day trip destination in Dresden. People went to "Findlater's" for a cup of coffee, a glass of wine, a chat with good friends. In 1849, Findlater's vineyard was purchased by Prince Albrecht of Prussa, the brother of the Prussian kings Friedrich Wilhelm IV and Wilhelm I. He had the palace and guest house demolished, and in its place he had a new large palace built for himself and his mistress, Baroness Rosalie von Rauch, by the Prussian state master builder Adolph Lohse, a pupil of Schinkel. After his divorce, the Hohenzollern prince was forced to move to the neighbouring kingdom of Saxony to avoid being in full daily view of Berlin society and thus compromising the Prussian royal family.

The park on the slope of the Elbe and by Bautzener Strasse was designed in the Lenné style, but it was only made accessible to the public in 1930. At the same time, Prince Albrecht also had a house built nearby for his head steward and chamberlain, von Stockhausen and his wife, although this house was smaller than the prince's own house. This estate, which was bought in 1891 by the sewing machine manufacturer Bruno Naumann, the owner of the world-famous company of Seidel & Naumann, was acquired in 1906 by Karl August Lingner, a

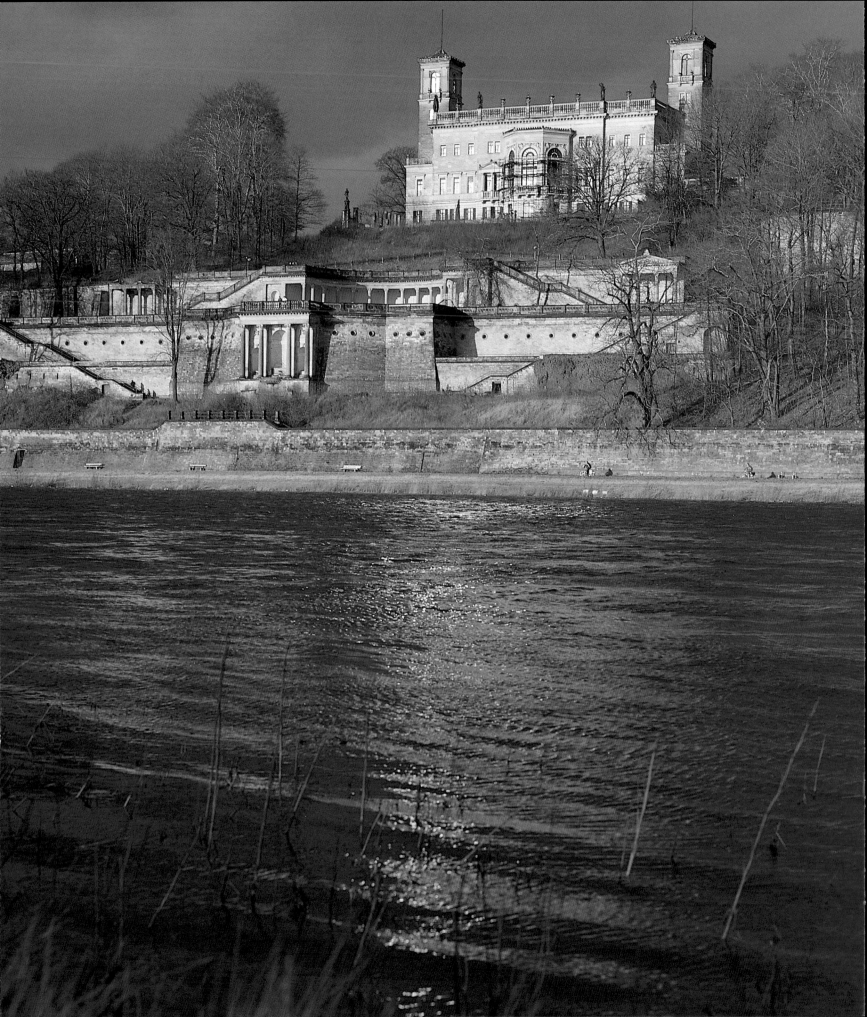

man who became rich by founding a pharmaceutic company in Dresden under the brand name of "Odol". Lingner was also associated with the first hygiene exhibition in Dresden in 1911 and the foundation of the Museum of Hygiene.

Villa Marie by the "Blaues Wunder" (Blue Wonder)

Opposite Loschwitz on the old city side, or on the "left bank", as those born in Dresden would say, is Blasewitz. The village was only incorporated into Dresden in 1921 after a long period of resistance. In the 19th century it had been a popular place for building summer residences and country houses. Building regulations issued in 1863 and 1876 soon made Blasewitz a site for villas built by high Dresden officials, businessmen and rich artists. Foreigners also chose Blasewitz as their permanent address and built villas there. Around 1870 they were also followed by the family of a Hungarian count. That was the origin of the Villa Marie, which is idyllically situated on the bank of the Elbe with a wonderful view of the Loschwitz bank of the Elbe, although this view was restricted twenty years later by the construction of the "Blue Wonder". In the last 25 years, this villa has played a special role in the artistic life of the city of Dresden:

"At the end of the 1970s mainly younger artists born in the 1950s began to find a form language which they put into practice independently of the requirements of cultural politics and without any striving for official recognition. Like the former painters of the "Brücke", they wanted to portray what they felt without any political censorship. At the same time, they latched on to the multimedia art forms of the 1920s and the social criticism of artistic expressions from the pre-war period. ... The decay of Dresden's buildings, ecological problems and interference with non-conforming artistic expressions by the representatives of official cultural policies were among the subjects of the activities with which these artists aimed to make people think and thus involve the public in their activities. ... At the end of the 1970s, artistic events already took place in private apartments and small galleries in Dresden which departed from academic art theory and ideological regulations, and were thus regarded with suspicion by the state censorship authorities, even when the intention of such activities was not political in any sense. ... Galeries which were known for such activities were the Leonhardi Museum, the residence gallery "fotogen" of Wanda C. Reichhardt in Villa Marie, the "Mitte" gallery and later the gallery of the Lehmann brothers which, in 1989, provided exhibition rooms for artists in a private apartment without state permission.

Wanda C. Reichert documented the activities of these Avant-Garde galleries, which constantly encountered resistance from official state bodies, in an art book which was published in 1989 under the title "chronisch 1" and which contained photographs of these galleries. In honour of the Villa Marie, which housed the gallery "fotogen" for almost ten years (before it was allocated, under highly questionable circumstances, to the state combine for fruit, vegetables and potatoes), Wanda C. Reichardt organised an artists' portfolio in which six artists gave expression to their involvement with the villa by the Elbe."

This characterisation of the extraordinary inner identity of the house was written by Helgard Sauer in her chapter "Desillusionierende Ansichten von Dresden" (Disillusioned views of Dresden), which appeared in the book "Dresden. Stadt der Fürsten – Stadt der Künstler" (Dresden. City of dukes – city of artists), Bergisch Gladbach 1991, P. 229 – 239.

View of Oberloschwitz

With Loschwitz, Dresden has a suburb which is unique, attractive and rich in history. Between 1803 and 1835, the Berlin architect Karl Friedrich Schinkel often visited Dresden and sometimes stayed for several weeks. In August 1829 after a stay at a health centre in Karlsbad, he also spent some time here. He went on trips to the romantic Plauen valley, to Tharandt and Weesenstein. His accommodation was in Loschwitz, about which he wrote in a leter: "With real pleasure and under the beneficial effects I am staying here in your splendid scenic area, which is something that can be wished

Villa Marie by the "Blaues Wunder"
(Blue Wonder)

View of Oberloschwitz

for a poor Berliner. I look with longing at every small vineyard in Loschwitz and ask myself whether it is a place where one can retire from a hectic life. Hopes and scenes like this have a healing power, and I keep myself open to them in order to take a good quantity back with me to Berlin to sustain me in our desert." But in spite of this, Schinkel did not come to Dresden when he was offered the professorship of architecture at the Dresden art college and building academy in 1833.

The vineyards and wine taverns which Ludwig Richter wrote of and recorded in pictures are no longer there. Instead, the slope of the Elbe from the former Loschwitz village square, now known as Körnerplatz up to Oberloschwitz is dotted with small houses and villas. Since the turn of the century there has been a suspended cable car from Pillnitzer Strasse to the Loschwitz height, overcoming a height difference of 84 metres in a distance of 280 metres. It was the first suspended passenger cable car route in Europe. Since 6th May 1901, passengers have been able to enjoy the trip past 33 iron structures to the hilltop, from where there is a splendid view over the Elbe valley, to the hills of "Little Switzerland" in Saxony and Bohemia, to the eastern Erzgebirge and, in clear weather, even to the central Bohemian mountains. It is still a worthwhile excursion to visit Loschwitz, enjoy the Elbe scenery and go to the hilltop to enjoy the wide expanse of the Saxon landscape.

The "Blaues Wunder" (Blue Wonder)

Upstream along the Elbe, a bold steel structure spreading across the Elbe can be seen from afar. It is the next bridge upstream from the Albertbrücke in Dresden and the bridge which has, since 1st April 1921, linked the Dresden suburbs of Blasewitz and Loschwitz and, at the same time, provided an access route to the city centre from the east. The first plans for a bridge here were made in 1872/83, but they were not pursued any further for lack of money. At the beginning of the 1880s, the plans were brought out again and two designs were commissioned, one by the established bridge-building engineers of the Königin-Marien-Hütte (Queen Mary Steelworks) in Cainsdorf near Zwickau, the other by the Carlswerk in Mühlheim on the Rhine. The Loschwitz council set up an Elbe bridge association for the purpose to promote the activities necessary to prepare the construction of the bridge. The Saxon Ministry of Finance and the waterways authority formulated conditions for the bridge construction project. In cooperation with the bridge construction specialist in the Saxon Ministry of Finance, Professor Köpcke, the Cainsdorf company revised its plans, submitted an offer for the execution of the building work and was granted the commission after it had submitted the best priced proposal. The largest iron, steel and furnace company of the 19th century in Saxony began construction work on the "Blue Wonder" in 1891. It was the

1500th bridge to be built by the Cainsdorf metalworking company. In June 1893 the bridge, with its structure which was unusual at the time for Saxony, as completed. The stress testing was carried out on 11th July 1893 when vehicles and loads weighing a total of about 157 tonnes were moved onto the bridge. A few days later, a company of the Saxon infantry had to march in step over the bridge to test the effect of the vibrations, which can severely endanger the stability of a bridge. When this test had also passed without any problems, the bridge was formally opened for public traffic on 17th July 1893. After 1900, about 300 trams per day crossed the bridge on the route to Pillnitz, and over 300 cars passed over the bridge so that it soon needed to be widened – which had already been taken into account in the design of the bridge. But it was only in 1934 that the carriageway of the "Blue Wonder" was widened to 10.20 metres. In the spring of 1945, preparations were made to blow up the bridge, but destruction was prevented by the master fitter Erich Stöckel and the telegraph worker Paul Zickler who cut the detonation cable. A memorial panel at the Blasewitz end of the bridge commemorates this courageous deed of two citizens of Dresden in the last few days of the Second World War.

Both after the First World War and after the Second World War, no regular maintenance work was carried out on the bridge and, in particular, the necessary annual coat of paint – which had given the bridge its name – was not applied. The usefulness of the bridge suffered accordingly. Tram transport on the bridge was discontinued on 10th April 1985. After extensive preservation work, the bridge is now reserved for private car transport only, and thus there is a good chance that this steel bridge structure, which has existed for over 100 years, can be preserved.

View towards Wachwitz and the television tower

The Dresden television tower on Wachwitz height can be seen from a long way off in the surrounding countryside. With its height of 252 metres, it has been a new symbol of Dresden since it was first taken into service in 1969. Below the television tower is Wachwitz with its quiet streets and small houses dating from the 18th century. There are also larger villas, the largest of which is the royal villa. The building was built in its present form in 1892 and 1893. From 1894 to the end of the monarchy in Saxony it was the summer residence of the royal family from King Albert and King Georg up to the time of the popular figure of King Friedrich August III.

Prince Friedrich August, who was born in 1797, bought two vineyards in 1824, and others were acquired in the period up to 1853. Together, they made up the "royal vineyard" of Wachwitz, and with the associated buildings they belonged to the Albertine Wettins. In 1936/37, Schloss Wachwitz (Wachwitz Palace) was built almost at the top of the hill, and Margrave Friedrich Christian lived in it with his family until 1945. In the land reform in the Soviet Occupation Zone, the family was dispossessed along with all owners of estates of more than 100 hectares. As family members of the Albertine Wettins such as the Jesuit priest Prince Georg and Prince Ernst Heinrich were very close to the resistance movement against the National Socialists, the legality of the dispossession can at least be called into question.

After vineyard cultivation had been discontinued as a result of the vine pest attack, the slopes of the Elbe between Wachwitz and Pillnitz were planted with fruit trees towards the end of the 19th century. As these orchards were left uncultivated after 1918, it is now wooded and in places consists of dense standings of deciduous trees. Fruit cultivation still exists, with the appropriate research and training, in Pillnitz. On the terrain of the "royal vineyard" in Wachwitz, a rhododendron garden was planted in the 1960s and now attracts thousands of visitors each year, especially in May when the many different varieties of rhododendrons are in full bloom.

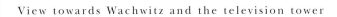
View towards Wachwitz and the television tower

Elbe scenery near Tolkewitz

Around the city

Pillnitz

For the festivities planned for June 1725 in Pillnitz on the occasion of the wedding of Auguste Constantia, the daughter of August the Strong from his liaison with Anna Constantia Countess Cosel, to the chief master falconer Heinrich Friedrich Count of Friesen, the Privy Secretary and court bookkeeper Weidemann composed a unique eulogy on Schloss Pillnitz (Pillnitz Palace):

"The pleasant and noteworthy Pillnitz 1725"

"Thou pleasant place, Thou worldly paradise, / Thou dost please my king above all others, / What pleasure I find within Thy beautiful walls. / May heaven bid time to tarry. / If I regard the scene, the silver river, / Which Saxon's Neptune must call Master, / Full forest shade I find upon the shore, / The beasts go by in fertile rich fields. / Turning around, I see the pleasure place of Bacchus, / The mountains with their rich adornment, / Like an amphitheatre pointing up white steps, / In short, all is incomparable here. / If I behold the garden, what a rare play, / For pleasure and joy is the goal here, / And dark melancholy is not allowed, / When I tread the bank, all care must flee, / But I hesistate and remain standing, / One must especially enter the rooms / Where Venus' court from Saxony and Poland resides, / The eye holds back and I say it freely / The heart feels it and you will not / Be free from this torment as soon as

you think, / So leave; But what must I see, / Which can highly delight the insensitive. / Look at the goddess in all her beauty, / Who, say you, is honoured as the fairest here? / With me and all others I know you will say, / What is seen in Versailles can also be asked for here. / But this is the greatest pleasure and beauty of the place, / My most gracious August, my king lives here!"

At this time, the place which was first mentioned in a document in 1335 as "Belenewitz", with its manor house first mentioned in 1350, had only been owned by the Elector for thirty years. In 1420 it had passed from the burgraviate of Dohna to the margraviate of Meissen, and the lands of Pillnitz, which in the 17th century included the villages of Hosterwitz, Krieschendorf, Pappritz, Borsberg, Wachwitz, Oberpoyritz, Graupa, Söbrigen, Niederpoyritz, Birkwitz, Wünschendorf and Bennewitz, had been taken over by families of the Saxon nobility which were closely linked with the court in Dresden, some of them because of their offices at court. After long negotiations, the young Elector finally acquired them from the von Bünau family in 1693 in exchange for the Lichtenwalde lands near Chemnitz, and in January 1694 he gave the manor house as a gift to his mistress Magdalena Sybilla von Neitschütz, the Imperial Countess of Rochlitz, whom he loved above all else. When both died of smallpox three months later, the new Elector Friedrich August I confiscated the property and leased it to Wolf

The open-air steps to the Elbe by the
Wasserpalais (Water Palace) in Pillnitz

Rudolph von Carlowitz, gave it as a pledge to his mother, the Electoral widow Anna Sophia of Denmark, exchanged it again in 1702 for the Ostra estate and sold it in the same year to a widowed Frau von Einsiedel. Anna Sophie bought it back from her in 1706 and gave it to her son, who immediately gave it to his mistress, Anna Constantia von Cosel. When she fell into disgrace in 1715 and was finally banished to Stolpen, the Elector/king took it under his own administration in 1718. Thereafter it remained with the Electoral family. The manor estate became a courtly estate, the palace was converted into a summer residence.

From 1720 to 1721, the Elector/king commissioned von Pöppelmann to build the water palace with the broad arching outdoor stairs watched over by two sphinxes as a landing place for gondolas. (An elegant red gondola, such as those used for trips from Dresden to Pillnitz, has been on display in the park since 1956.) Two years later, the Bergpalais (Hill palace) was built as a mirror image. In between was the old palace with four wings, which burned down in 1818 and in place of which Christian Friedrich Schurricht built the Neues Palais (New Palace) from 1818 to 1826 in a style similar to the water palace and the hill palace. Even today, the Chinese style roof structure is impressive, as are the Chinese paintings in the broad grooves, which were uncovered and restored from 1964 onwards: red on yellow in the side buildings, blue on red in the central structure and blue in the porch of the water palace.

The extensive reconstruction of the Pillnitz palace complex also included the commission given to head state master builder Pöppelmann in 1725 to construct a wide avenue of chestnut trees from the palace to Hosterwitz on the way to Dresden. When the palace is approached via this avenue, which is as beautiful in spring as it is in autumn, we gain a unique impression of its tranquility and its majestic size, the unity of the unspoiled scenery, the artistically designed park and the architecture.

August the Strong sometimes used Pillnitz Palace as a setting for festivals and entertainments, and in 1695 he once used it as a background for a farming costume event, and did so more frequently in the 1720s, for example in 1721, 1723, 1724 and 1725. In 1728, the Saxon Elector and his visitors, King Friedrich Wilhelm I and his son, Crown Prince Friedrich, stopped at Pillnitz on their way to the Königstein. The summer festival in Pillnitz, which was usually held in July and August for two or three weeks, must have been extremely entertaining, especially because the court society always invented new ideas. In the "diversions" in the first week of August 1721, there was a water shooting event on the garden pond on the morning of 7th August. The target was on one long side of the rectangular pond, and the shooters took up their position on the oppo-

site side. They had to shoot onto the surface of the water in such a way that the bullet hit the target. Besides the Elector/king, the members of the royal family had to take part in this event, i.e. the Electoral Prince, the Duke of Württtemberg, the Duke of Weissenfels and the Elector/king's closest confidants and ministers. At the end of the shooting event, in which August the Strong and his son Friedrich August jointly won second place, there was a particular entertainment which is recorded in the files of the chief chamberlain's office: "The chief courtier, Count von Königsegg and the Privy Cabinet Minister Count Vitzthumb were obliged to give up their shoes, the former because he had missed all six stages of the event and the latter because he had not shot his bullets onto the water but directly into the target. These shoes were nailed to the target and all the shooters shot at them." We can be sure that these elegant shoes were no longer fit to wear after this treatment.

After the reign of August the Strong, only the court festivities of 1738 and 1747 at weddings achieved a certain importance. From 1765, Pillnitz became the permanent summer residence of the Electoral family, which became the royal family from 1806. The ruler moved to Pillnitz in May/June with his family and all his court, and he only moved back into Dresden Palace during September. Therefore, Pillnitz Palace is associated with important events in Saxon, Ger-

The Wasserpalais (Water Palace) in Pillnitz

View from the Maillebahn (Maille railway)
to the Neues Palais (New Palace)

The Palm House before renovation

man and European history. From 25th to 27th August 1791, Emperor Leopold II and King Friedrich Wilhelm II of Prussia were in Pillnitz with Count Artois, the brother of King Louis XVI of France. They negotiated about possible joint policies towards Poland and France. The Pillnitz Declaration witnessed their interest in the full restoration of the power of the king in revolutionary France, and it finally led to the war of the Empire against France. When Napoleon came to Pillnitz in 1812, he could rightly say: "This is where I was born!" In the autumn of 1849 after the bourgeouis revolution in Germany, the Austrian Emperor Franz Joseph and the Prussian King Friedrich Wilhelm IV accepted Saxon hospitality to consult about the continuation of the German League after the removal of the Frankfurt national assembly, the draft constitution for the Empire and the central government. In 13th September 1830 Bernhard August von Lindenau (appointed as a cabinet minister after the resignation of Einsiedel), von Könneritz, Dr. Gruner and a number of other influential people went to Pillnitz, described to King Anton the political situation with the September riots and obtained his signature for the nomination of Prince Friedrich August, who was regarded as progressive, as his co-ruler. This represented the official step towards a constitutional monarchy and a bourgouis constitutional state in Saxon.

Pillnitz is also known far beyond the borders of Saxony because of its unique park complex. Dresden's honorary citizen Fritz Löffler wrote: "In no other gardens near Dresden can the development of landscape architecture be traced as completely as in Pillnitz. Of the French garden complex, only the arbours, the hedge gardens and the Maille railway are preserved. … By adding further land towards the hills and the village around 1780 next to the French garden, it was possible to create an English garden which reaches well beyond the garden as far as the dramatic scenery of Friedrichsgrund at the Bordberg hill. And finally the third period, the scientific period of the 19th century, subjected the garden to strict dendrological purposes. … The landscape garden was not removed, but it was filled with such foreign trees and shrubs as were catalogued, labelled with their Latin names and scientifically classified…"

The most famous trees in the park undoubtedly include the camelia with a height of eight metres and a treetop circumference of 35 metres, which was brought from Japan with three other plants of its kind in 1770 and given to the leading gardens of the time in London, Paris, Hannover and Pillnitz. It bears pink blossoms at the end of April and the beginning of May after it has survived the Saxon winter in a specially constructed winter house which is fitted over the tree. The park also includes an Orangerie building, the middle section of which was built by Longuelune in 1730. When the adjacent terrain to the north was added to the park in 1785, Elector Friedrich August III had a Dutch garden designed in which plants from South Africa were planted. In 1859, a palm house was also erected for this purpose. This palm house detriorated in the 1970s, but it can now be admired in its old splendour again.

The Baroque Garden of Großsedlitz

With the Baroque garden of Großsedlitz situated half way from Dresden to Königstein fortress on the left bank of the Elbe, Saxony has the most complete example of a French park. In 1719, the cabinet minister Graf August Christoph von Wackerbarth acquired the manor estate of Großsedlitz on which the manor building had been destroyed by a fire in 1715. Wackerbarth, who was born in 1662 and came from Lauenburg, had become the general director and chief inspector of all civil and military buildings in Electoral Saxony under August the Strong as early as 1696. Alongside Graf Flemming, he was one of the most influential political advisors and ministers of the Wettin ruler. He did good work creating a systematic structure for the state building office. Under his leadership and with the master builders and architects of the state building office, i. e. Pöppelmann, Longuelune, Knöffel, Karcher and Le Plat, basically those buildings arose which dominate the visual character of the

Großsedlitz Baroque Garden

Großsedlitz Park with Friedrichschlösschen (Friedrich Palace)

127

Dresden city centre and the palaces of the Dresden residence city today. Like the other ministers, Wackerbarth was also a building owner. After he had become Governor of Dresden, he commissioned Johann Christoph Knöffel to build the Gouvernmentshaus (government house), the later Kurländisches Palais. There followed the palace park complex of Großsedlitz, Wackerbarth's place of peace in Hoflössnitz, and in 1728 Zabeltitz with the splendid park, a site of noble Baroque culture which was outstanding in the Augustine age. Wackerbarth built for four years in Großsedlitz, then August the Strong purchased the complex from him, but kept the change of ownership secret until 1726. The three-wing palace complex known as the Friedrichschlösschen (Friedrich Palace) was never really finished. In the Seven Years War it served for a time as the headquarters of Friedrich the Great, was destroyed in 1813 and demolished in 1871, and then the building that is now on this site was built. Original buildings preserved from the Augustine era are the Orangerie, the stairs, the garden design and the numerous sculptures by Coudray, Kirchner and Thomae. Until 1756, the Dresden court celebrated the donation of the White Eagle Order by August the Strong in 1705.

Weesenstein Palace and park

In the narrow Müglitz valley, far removed from trunk roads and the mass of tourists, on a hill spur jutting out into the valley on the way to the eastern Erzgebirge is Schloss Weesenstein (Weesenstein Palace). Until 1402 it was an important part of the burgraviate of Dohna, which already maintained a fortress here in the 13th century, and then it passed to the margraves of Meissen and was given by them to the von Bünau family. This family then owned Weesenstein until 1772 and undertook systematic building work on its feudal property. The fortress became a palace in the 16th century, and further building work on the palace was carried out in the 17th, 18th and 19th century. After the palace and land rights of Weesenstein had been in the possession of the family von Bünau for over 360 years, Rudolf von Bünau had to sell the property in 1772 out of financial necessity as a result of the Seven Years War. It was finally purchased by King Anton for 325,000 Talers as a private possession for the Wettin family. The aged ruler retired to Weesenstein especially after the riots of 1830/31 and their effects. When Anton died childless in 1836, it was inherited by his brother Maximilian, who was only a few years younger and was the father of King Friedrich August II and his younger brother Johann. The latter inherited it from his father in 1838. For Prince Johann, the King of Saxony from 1854 to 1873, Weesenstein became one of his favourite places to stay. Johann lived in the palace for several weeks in the spring and autumn, received high visitors, worked uninterrupted on his translation of Dante and on his memoirs, political tracts, draft laws and speeches to the state parliament. On his last visit to Weesenstein, King Friedrich August II wrote in Johann's visitors book on 18th April 1854, only a few months before his tragic fatal accident near Brennbüchel in Tirol: "O Weesenstein! O Weesenstein. Thou art like a fairy tale in the moonlight, surrounded by dancing giants and dwarfs. the green valleys and hills. Several high houses called thee theirs. Thou white, slim fairy maid before the ducal emblem was espied at this outlook post. May the emblem forever green reach into your high bushy branch and may it flourish and grow to the blessing and joy of Saxony."

After the First World War, the Wettins sold the palace and estate to a manufacturing family, but this family was also not able to maintain the property. In 1934 it was acquired by the Saxon local history protection association for 30,000 Reich marks and set up as a museum. In the Second World War it was a temporary storage place for the treasures from the Dresden art collections, and from 1943 for works of art collected from the whole of Europe at Hitler's command which were planned to be included in "Linz Führer Museum" as a "World Museum". No wonder that the palace became an important centre of attention for the personnel of the Soviet trophy commission after 8th May 1945.

Weesenstein Palace has been owned by the Free State of Saxony since 1992. It is not

Schloss Weesenstein (Weesenstein Palace)

The park of Schloss Weesenstein
(Weesenstein Palace)

only a worthwhile excursion destination in attractive scenery and a place with an interesting Saxon history – it is also an increasingly popular site for scientific events.

Moritzburg

In the middle of a large forest area known as the Friedewald to the north-east of Dresden there is a hunting palace which is well known throughout Europe and even further afield: Moritzburg. The palace took its name from the person who built it. In 1542, a year after he had become the reigning duke of the Albertine ducal state of Saxony, the twenty-one year old Moritz had a fortified hunting palace built, and to maintain it he set up the Moritzburg office. The fortress-type complex also gave a new name to the nearby community of Eisenberg. Up to the end of the 17th century it was a base for Electoral hunts. To increase the "yield" of such hunts, the largest part of the Friedwald forest was developed as an animal reserve after 1661 and surrounded by a high wall. Elector Johann Georg IV had the hunting area adapted for course hunting. His younger brother Friedrich August I, who succeeded him as the ruler, continued this practice. Soon, the dukes were concerned with plans to modernise and extend the hunting palace, but these plans could only be carried out after 1720. Again it was Pöppelmann who constructed a monumental palace building for his ruler in the years up

to 1727. The palace was situated on an island in a regulated pond, a main avenue from Dresden leads in a straight line to the palace. Four large round towers surround the weighty central building, which is reached by a comfortable drive ramp because the whole of the palace is on a large, artificial terrace. Moritzburg was very popular with the Saxon monarchs as a place to stay. After 1918, in the law on the property dispute between the house of Wettin and the Free State of Saxony, Moritzburg Hunting Palace was awarded to the Wettins as private property. They lived there until 1945, when they fled to Bavaria before the advancing Red Army troops.

After the death of August the Strong, Moritzburg was not visited so often by the Dresden court. Elector Friedrich August II preferred Hubertusburg, which he had converted to a second residence. It was only Elector Friedrich August III, the son of Friedrich Christian, who again turned to Pillnitz and Moritzburg. In 1769, construction work began on the new pheasant palace, the two-storey building with the striking dome-type roof structure which reminds the beholder of Pillnitz. A mandarin is seated on the lantern which completes the roof and is protected with a parasol by a servant. The figure turns with the wind – an imaginative and humourous feature. The pheasant palace was no longer used for representation purposes, but rather for comfortable, almost bourgeois and lowly residential purposes.

After 1770, the pheasant palace complex was supplemented on the large pond side by buildings which seem strange today. We see a lighthouse standing on a mole, and on the other bank are fortifications known as Dardanelles. This needs a few words of explanation. At that time, the Russian fleet under the command of an English admiral had just passed the Dardanelles in the war with the Ottoman Empire, an event which was generally known in Europe. The Saxon elector had an imitation of the panorama made, set up an Electoral Saxon shipbuilding yard there and had a miniature frigate built. With this royal toy, which was dismantled and disposed of 30 years later as a shipwreck, sea battles and pirate games were held on the large pond. "But the complex with its miniature palace and the lighthouse that was never used, the imitation fortifications and the toy ship for big children were admired at that time as a wonder. They matched the taste of the times, as the benevolent echo of many portrayals shows. … Here in the peace and quiet, only occasionally interrupted by the theatrical spectacle of imaginary sea battles, this was where the family life of Friedrich August III took place. … But in the last resort this was an escape from the reality of society into a playful and sentimental make-believe world…" The monarchy has passed. What remains is the architectural heritage in a unique landscape which is a constant attraction for contemplation, excursions and walks.

Fasanenschlösschen (Pheasant Palace)
in Moritzburg

Meissen

The Meissen Burgberg, Albrechtsburg and cathedral rise up majestically above the Elbe and are visible far and wide. In German history, this Meissen is a symbol of the rule of worldly and spiritual powers, of the permanent gain of the geographical area between the Saale, Elbe, Oder and Queis, of the development of the dominion of state, of richness, creativity and the spirit. The name of Meissen stands for the Wettin regional state, for church organisation, for the municipality and also for the artistic, cultural and scientific elements in the form of porcelain, for spiritual enjoyment with good wine. Even in the 18th century, when the political entity of the Albertine Electorate of Saxony already had an influence on German and European development, people still spoke of Meissen when they were referring to Saxony. In the 20th volume of Zedler's universal lexicon of 1739, Meissen is "one of the most beautiful states in Germany".

After the successful battle against the Daleminzi in the spring of 929, Heinrich's army proceeded as far as the Elbe. This is reported three quarters of a century later by Bishop Thietmar von Merseburg in his "Chronicle": "At the Elbe, he had buildings erected on a hill which at that time was densely covered with trees. Here, he created the fortress to which he gave the name of Meissen, after a stream which flowed to the north of it. He gave it troops and fortifications such as are normal today. From there, he forced the Milzi poeple, who were subjected to his reign, to pay tribute." Thus, Meissen became the starting point for Saxon history.

The admirable city archivist of many years wrote the following thoughts on the occasion of the city's 1000th anniversary in his history of the city, which is still unsurpassed: "The writer of history who has to portray a great occurrence or development is like a world traveller. He collects thousands of individual impressions, each valuable in its own way, but his overall task often forces him to condense the small and special into the great, or to omit it altogether for the sake of the overall picture. The portrayal of the history of a city particularly demands this, even if for long period it is associated with the glamour of historic greatness, of festivities and the rich, like Meissen. … Nothing in Saxony can claim to have such varied and yet such far-reaching importance, and yet few towns have suffered from such hindering powers and such destructive phenomena as Meissen. But it is this very tension between such widely differing elements which have given its past the dynamism which has made its name known and valuable to both the academic memory and to the popular and historical memory. … So let the work be finished. If it fully supports the insight in our land that history is the great teacher of mankind, if it stimulates those who read it to contemplation and a historical perspective, then its purpose is fulfilled and it can claim, as we read of the prophet Ezekiel: 'Behold, I went through the realm of the past, but life is pulsing behind me!'"

Literature

This bibliography only includes titles which were directly used in the preparation of the text. For a complete bibliography of the history of Dresden, please refer to the 4–volume "Bibliographie zur Geschichte der Stadt Dresden", Dresden 1981.

Dresden. Silhouetten einer Stadt. (Dresden, Silhouette of a City), ed. Günter Klieme, 1st edition, Dresden 1985.

Dresden und seine berühmten Besucher. (Dresden and its Famous Visitors.) From documents of the Dresden Historical Association, 1892–1936, ed. Gerald Kolditz, Dresdner Hefte, special edition 1992.

Das Dresdener Schloss. Monument sächsischer Geschichte und Kultur. (Dresden Palace. A Monument of Saxon History and Culture.) 2nd revised edition, Dresden 1989.

Dresdner Hefte (Dresden Booklets): Repräsentation und Historismus. Dresden am Ende des 19. Jahrhunderts. (Representation and Historicism. Dresden at the End of the 19th Century), Vol. 9, No. 27, 1991.
Um die Vormacht im Reich. Christian I, sächsischer Kurfürst, 1586–1591. (For supremacy in the Empire. Christian I, Saxon Elector 1586–1591.) Vol. 10, No. 29, 1992.
Die Loschwitz-Pillnitzer Kulturlandschaft (The Cultivated Loschwitz-Pillnitz Area), Vol. 11, No. 34, 1994.
Reformdruck und Reformgesinnung. Dresden vor dem 1. Weltkrieg. (Pressure to Reform and Reform Consciousness. Dresden before the First World War.) Vol. 11, No. 36, 1993.
Die Moritzburger Kulturlandschaft (The Cultivated Moritzburg Area), Vol. 13, No. 42, 1995.
Zwischen Integration und Vernichtung. Jüdisches Leben in Dresden im 19. und 20. Jahrhundert. (Between Integration and Annihilation. Jewish Life in Dresden in the 19th and 20th Century.) Vol. 14, No. 45, 1996. Grosses Ostragehege / Friedrichstadt. Geschichte und Entwicklungschancen. (Large Ostra Estate / Friedrichstadt. History and Development Opportunities.) Vol. 14, No. 47, 1996.

Gross, Reiner: Die Residenz des sächsischen Königreiches in der bürgerlichen Umwälzung von 1840 bis 1871. (The Residence of the Saxon Kingdom in the Bourgeois Reform from 1840 to 1871.) Dresdner Hefte, Vol. 8, No. 24, 1990.

Gurlitt, Cornelius: Dresden, Berlin 1905. (Die Kultur. Ed. C. Curlitt, Vol. 23 and 24).

Haenel, Erich; Kalkschmidt, Eugen: Das alte Dresden. Bilder und Dokumente aus zwei Jahrhunderten. (Old Dresden. Pictures and Documents from Two Centuries.) Licence edition, Bindlach 1995.

Hahn, Alfred; Neef, Ernst: Dresden. Ergebnisse der heimatkundlichen Bestandsaufnahme. (Dresden. Results of Local Studies.), Berlin 1984. (Vol. 42 of Werte unserer Heimat / Treasures of our Home).

Hartmann, Hans-Günther: Moritzburg. Schloss und Umgebung in Geschichte und Gegenwart. (Moritzburg. Palace and Surrounding Area in Past and Present.) 2nd, revised edition, Weimar 1990.

Hartmann, Hans-Günther: Pillnitz. Schloss, Park und Dorf. (Pillnitz. Palace, Park and Village.) 3rd, revised edition, Weimar 1996.

Hennig, Lutz; Müller, Katja; Wintermann, Klaus-Dieter: Weesenstein. 700 Jahre Schlossgeschichte. (Weesenstein. 700 Years of Palace History.) Dresden 1995.

Klecker, Christine: Johann von Sachsen und Schloss Weesenstein. (Johann of Saxony and Weesenstein Palace.) In: Sächsische Heimatblätter (Saxon Regional Periodical), Vol. 38, No. 1, 1992, P. 53–57.

Löffler, Fritz: Das alte Dresden. Geschichte seiner Bauten. (Old Dresden. History of its Buildings.) 13th, revised edition, Leipzig 1997.

Magirius, Heinrich. Das zweite Dresdner Hoftheater Gottfried Sempers und die Theatralisierung von Architektur und Bildenden Künsten des späten Historismus in Dresden. (The Second Dresden Court Theatre of Gottfried Semper and the Theatralisation of Architecture and the Visual Arts of Late Historicism in Dresden.) In: Repräsentation und Historismus. Dresden am Ende des 19. Jahrhunderts. (Representation and Historicism. Dresden at the End of the 19th Century), Dresdner Hefte, Vol. 9, No. 27, 1991.

May, Walter: Der Prozess gegen den Grafen Brühl. (The Trial of Count Brühl.) In: Sächsische Heimatblätter (Saxon Regional Periodical), Vol. 17, 1971.

Meinert, Günther: Zur Geschichte des Theaterbaues in Dresden. (The History of Theatre Construction in Dresden.) In: Sächsische Heimatblätter (Saxon Regional Periodical), Vol. 14, No. 5, 1968.

Mertens, Klaus: Barockgarten Großsedlitz. Ein Rundgang mit Orangerie, Stiller Musik und Aha. (Großsedlitz Baroque Garden. A Tour with Orangerie, Silent Music and Aha.) Pub.: State Palace Department, Großsedlitz Baroque Garden, 1995.

Nadler, Hans: Die katholische Hofkirche zu Dresden und ihr Wiederaufbau nach der Zerstörung am 13. Februar 1945. (The Catholic Court Church in Dresden and its Reconstruction after Destruction on 13th February 1945.) In: Sächsische Heimatblätter (Saxon Regional Periodical), Vol. 24, No. 6, 1978.

Nitzschke, Karin; Koch, Lotar: Dresden. Stadt der Fürsten – Stadt der Künstler. (Dresden. City of Dukes – City of Artists.) Bergisch Gladbach 1991.

Gottfried Semper zum 100. Todestag. (The 100th Anniversary of the Death of Gottfried Semper.) Exhibition Catalogue. Dresden 1979.

Schmidt, Gerhard: Dresden und seine Kirchen. (Dresden and its Churches.) A documentation, 3rd, revised edition. Berlin 1976.

Schumann, Paul: Dresden. Leipzig 1909.

700 Jahre politische Mitbestimmung in Sachsen. (700 Years of Political Representation in Saxony.) Ed. Karlheinz Blaschke. Dresden 1994.

Stüting, Manfred G.: Der schönste Milchladen der Welt. Dresdner Molkerei Gebrüder Pfund. (The Most Beautiful Milk Shop in the World. The Dresden Dairy of the Pfund Brothers.) Dresden 1996.

Wintermann, Klaus-Dieter: König Johann von Sachsen. Lebenswerk – Zeit. (King Johann of Saxony. His Life's Work and Times.) In: Sächsische Heimatblätter (Saxon Regional Periodical), Vol. 38, No. 1, 1992, P. 1f.

Zimmermann, Ingo: Zur Charakteristik der Persönlichkeit Johanns von Sachsen. (A Characterisation of the Personality of Johann of Saxony.) Sächsische Heimatblätter (Saxon Regional Periodical), Vol. 38, No. 1, 1992, P. 3–6.

Index

Index of names

Albert (1828 – 1902), King of Saxony 13, 20, 22, 115

Albrecht (1443 – 1500), Duke of Saxony 12, 18

Albrecht (1809 – 1872), Prince of Prussia 107

Andersen, Hans Christian (1805 – 1875), Danish writer 92

Anna of Denmark (1532 – 1585) Electress of Saxony 75, 120

Anton (the Kind) (1755 – 1836), King of Saxony 124, 128

Aristotle (384 – 322 BC), Greek philosopher 23

Arnold von Westfalen (d. 1480), Master Builder 18

Artois, Count (1757 – 1836), brother of King Louis XVI of France 124

August (1526 – 1586), Elector of Saxony 18, 26, 74, 96

Bähr, George (1666 – 1738), Council Carpenter 25, 34, 42, 98

Bähr, Johann Karl 20

Bakunin, Michael Alexandrovich (1814 – 1876), Russian revolutionary 78

Balestra, Pietro (d. after 1729), Italian sculptor 72

Beethoven, Ludwig van (1770 – 1827), composer 62

Bendemann, Eduard (1811 – 1889), historical painter 43

Bernini, Lorenzo (1598 – 1680), Italian master builder and sculptor 18

Beust, Friedrich Ferdinand von (1809 – 1886), Saxon Foreign Minister 71

Beutler, Gustav Otto (1853 – 1926), Mayor of Dresden 67

Bienert, Traugott (1813 – 1896), mill owner 82

Boccum, Ursula Katharina von (1680 – 1730), Countess Lubormirska, Duchess of Teschen, mistress of August the Strong 75, 79

Bodt, Jean de (1670 – 1745), architect 51, 96

Böttger, Johann Friedrich (1682 – 1719), chemist and co-inventor of European hard porcelain 96

Borromini, Francesco (1599 – 1667), Italian architect 18

Bouché, Julius Carl Friedrich (1850 – 1944) landscape architect, Head Gardener in Dresden 72

Bräther, Edmund (1855 – 1925), architect and Councillor for Building 67

Brühl, Heinrich Reichsgraf von (1700 – 1763), Saxon Prime Minister, 39, 42, 75, 78

Bünau, Rudolf von 128

Carlowitz, Wolf Rudolph von 120

Casanova, Giovani Battista (1728 – 1795), painter, Director of the Dresden Academy of Arts 79

Charles XII (1682 – 1718), King of Sweden 34, 51

Chiaveri, Gaetano (1689 – 1770), Italian architect 32, 34

Christian August (1666 – 1725) Duke of Saxony Zeitz, Bishop of Raab 32

Christian I (1560 – 1591), Elector of Saxony 26, 30, 74

Conert, Dr. Herbert (1886 – 1946) 11

Cosel, Anna Constantia Reichsgräfin von (1680 – 1765), mistress of August the Strong 36, 118, 120

Cosel, Anna Constantia Gräfin von (1708 – 1728), daughter of August the Strong 118

Coudray, François (1678 – 1727), sculptor 128

Crafft, Johann Daniel (1624 – 1697), manufacturer 75

Daleminzi, Slavic tribe 135

Dante Alighieri (1265 – 1321), Italian poet 63

Dehn-Rothfelser, Hans von (1500 – 1561), master fortress builder 26

Despléchin, Edouard Désiré Joseph 62

Devrient, Eduard (1801 – 1877), actor and producer 62

Diéterle, Jules Michel 62

Dietrich (the Oppressed) (1162 – 1221), Margrave of Meissen 16

Diez, Robert (1844 – 1922), sculptor 98

Dilich, Wilhelm (1571 – 1655), Head Master Builder, architect and artist 18

Dinglinger, Johann Melchior (1664 – 1731), goldsmith 51

Donndorf, Adolf von (1835 – 1916), sculptor 23

Dyck, Anton van (1599 – 1641), Dutch painter 28

Edler, Tobias (around 1685), cabinet maker 96

Einsiedel, Detlev Graf von (1773 – 1861), cabinet minister 43, 74, 120, 124

Elisabeth I (1533 – 1603), Queen of England 30

Emser, Hieronymus (1477 – 1527) court chaplain of Duke Georg of Saxony 23

Eosander, Johann Friedrich von, known as Göthe (around 1670 – 1729), architect, master fortress builder 85

Erlwein, Hans (1872 – 1914), architect, Councillor of Building 34, 49, 63, 85

Ermisch, Hubert (1883 – 1951), architect 58

Ernst (1441 – 1486), Elector of Saxony 12, 18

Ernst Heinrich (1896 – 1971), Prince of Saxony 115

Fehre, Johann Gottfried (1685 – 1753), Council Master Mason 98

Findlater, Jacob Lord of (1747 – 1811), Scottish peer 107

Flemming, Jakob Heinrich Graf von (1667 – 1728), master cabinet maker 25, 96, 124

Forberger, printer in Nürnberg 12

Francesco III (1698 – 1780), Duke of Modena 28

Franz I (1768 – 1835), Emperor of Austria (as Franz II: Roman-German Emperor until 1830) 13

Franz Joseph I (1830 – 1916), Emperor of Austria 124

Franz, Gerhard (born 1916), architecture historian 71

Frederick IV (1671 – 1730), King of Denmark 34, 50, 51

Friedrich II (the Serious) (1310 – 1349), Margrave of Meissen 20, 101

Friedrich II (the Meek) (1412 – 1464), Elector of Saxony 18, 36

Friedrich III (the Wise) (1463 – 1525), Elector of Saxony 20

Friedrich II (the Great) (1712 – 1786), King of Prussia 42, 78, 128

Friedrich August I (1670 – 1733), Elector of Saxony and King of Poland, called August the Strong 13, 18, 28, 30, 32, 34, 36, 38, 50, 51, 58, 72, 74, 75, 78, 85, 92, 96, 98, 101, 118, 120, 124, 128, 131

Friedrich August II (1696 – 1763), Elector of Saxony and King of Poland 28, 30, 32, 34, 36, 48, 50, 51, 85, 120, 131

Friedrich August III (the Just) (1750 – 1827), Elector of Saxony, also King Friedrich August I of Saxony 63, 68, 131

Friedrich August II (1797 – 1854), King of Saxony 13, 42, 88, 115, 124, 128

Friedrich August III (1865 – 1932), King of Saxony until 1918 75, 115, 124, 135

Friedrich Christian (1722 – 1763), Elector of Saxony 75, 131